Graphic Wit

THE ART OF HUMOR IN DESIGN

TEVEN HELLER & GAIL ANDERSON

WATSON-GUPTILL PUBLICATIONS NEW YORK

THIS BOOK IS DEDICATED TO
NICOLAS GIANNI HELLER,
WHO TAUGHT ME THAT CHILD'S PLAY
IS HARD WORK.

First published in 1991 by Watson-Guptill Publications, a division of
BPI Communications, Inc., 1515 Broadway, New York, N.Y. 10036

Edited by Paul Lukas
Senior Editor: Candace Raney
Art Direction: Louise Fili
Design: Lee Bearson
Computer Layout: Andrea Ross
Lettering: Steven Guarnaccia
Graphic Production: Ellen Greene
Text set in 11-point Sabon

Library of Congress Cataloging-in-Publication Data

Heller, Steven.
    Graphic wit: the art of humor in design/Steven Heller and Gail
Anderson.
       p.   cm.
    Includes index.
    ISBN 0-8230-2161-0 :
    1. Graphic arts—United States—Humor. 2. American wit and
humor, pictorial. I. Anderson, Gail, 1962–   . II. Title.
NC998.5A1H44 1991
741.6—dc20

Manufactured in Singapore

First printing, 1991

2 3 4 5 6 7 8 9 / 95 94 93 92

ACKNOWLEDGMENTS

Thanks to the many designers and illustrat[ors]
who allowed their work to be shown in this v[ol-]
ume. Special thanks to those interviewed, [for]
their patience and generosity.

Without the support of our friends [at]
Watson-Guptill, this book would have be[en]
impossible, so thanks to my Editor, Cand[ace]
Raney; Executive Editor Mary Suffudy; Prod[uc-]
tion Manager Ellen Greene; and Associate Ed[itor]
Paul Lukas, who has shepherded this project w[ith]
care and skill, keeping his wits and wit throu[gh-]
out while giving invaluable advice and direction[.]

To Louise Fili, for her format and art dir[ec-]
tion, 100 tips of the hat. To Steven Guarnacc[ia,]
for his cover illustration, 30 tips of the hat. [To]
Lee Bearson, associate designer and the backb[one]
of the design and production of this book, hea[rt]-
felt thanks—while he can never be repaid for [the]
many late, late nights, his place in Design Heav[en]
is now assured. To Bill Aller, for his additio[nal]
photography, the check's in the mail. To Lu[cy]
Carson, thanks for great stats. To Andrea Ros[s,]
who gamely consented to be the guinea pig in ou[r]
first experience with electronic paste-up, thank[s]
for many late hours of hard work and for easing
our transition into the digital world.

Many parties supported this endeavor. In
particular, heartfelt gratitude goes to Paul Rand,
Tom Bodkin, Fred Woodward, Martin Fox, James
Fraser, Caroline Hightower, Richard Wilde, and
Seymour Chwast, the best friend a guy could
want. And many thanks to Canon, for making a
copier that didn't break down at a critical time.

Finally, thanks to all those who make graphic wit and design humor, for they brighten up the
world of visual communications.—*SH & GA*

CONTENTS

WHAT'S SO FUNNY ABOUT GRAPHIC DESIGN?

IN THE BEGINNING WAS THE WORD

Actually, in the beginning there were paramecium. Then came pictures, and much later came words. But for purposes of developing the premise of this introduction, please allow me some latitude in condensing historical fact. This book is about words and images, and is repleat with word-packed sentences about how words and images coexist as unified entities—as ideas. This book is about a very special aspect of graphic design, which I call *graphic wit* or *design humor*. While not all graphic design is witty or humorous, humor serves to enliven all visual experience, particularly graphic communications. Not all designers possess the ability to create truly witty or humorous work, yet the desire to be endowed with this gift is probably universal. Although I pride myself on having a good sense of humor, sadly, I have never mastered the art of humor in design. Therefore, I have concluded that graphic wit takes unique talents and distinct powers, and merits this book-length examination—indeed, personal analysis—of work created by my peers and betters over the past decade. Working within an historical context, Gail Anderson and I compiled a wide stylistic and conceptual range of such work, with the sincere hope that by presenting some of the most clever, ironic, and acerbic pieces from annuals, exhibitions, and designer's drawers, something other than ink might rub off on us—and on you, if you're so inclined.

WELL-CHOSEN WORDS ON HUMOR

Despite Mark Twain's assertion that "a classic is something that everybody wants to have read and nobody wants to read," his works, most of them written a century ago, are classics that virtually everyone *has* read and are indelibly etched into our minds. Twain's masterpieces are memorable not only for their appealing characters and compelling tales, but for the brilliant humor that underscores every aspect of his anecdotal prose. Twain's uncommon sense of the absurd gave him the power to make his readers appreciate both the lighter and darker sides of human foible and folly. Humor was his weapon and truth his shield, and implicit in his writing is the idea that we are all fools, with Twain himself at the head of the procession. Indeed, this self-effacing spinner of yarns employed all types of wit and humor—from jest to satire, slapstick to irony—making vivid pastiches by intuitively incorporating just the right quantities of reality and fantasy into his curiously honest representations of the society in which he lived (and sometimes suffered). Today, Twain is a paradigm of American humor, and his work is a basis for my assertion that humor is one of the two most powerful weapons a society can wield for good or evil (the other being fear).

By now you are wondering, if this is a book about *graphic* wit and design humor, why I should begin with a paean to a writer. Well, in addition to the fact that Mr. Twain is one of my favorite American authors, his example proves my claim that wit and humor—a distinction that will be discussed in due time—are the most important ingredients in any creative stew, particularly for creativity that strives for memorability, like graphic or advertising design. Twain, like many of this country's greatest verbal and visual humorists, proves that humor is the key to overriding our complex, internal security systems. Humor lowers defenses, releases steam, and excites the mind. Humor adds dimension to our experience and gives us great latitude in human affairs. "Men will let you abuse them," wrote the nineteenth-century minister Henry Ward Beecher, "if only you will make them laugh."

In fact, humor's cousin, laughter, has quantifiable curative benefits. Norman Cousins, who in 1982 wrote about overcoming disease through daily doses of humor, says that laughter triggers a secretion into the brain of a mood-enhancing chemistry that staves off depression. "Laughter is higher than all pain," wrote the late-nineteenth-century designer and social reformer Elbert Hubbard. Of course, laughter is also symptomatic of other, less joyful, emotions: "Excess of sorrow laughs. Excess of joy weeps," wrote William Blake, and the poet Byron said ". . . if I laugh at any mortal thing,/'Tis that I may not weep."

This should not surprise us—since humor and laughter are cousins, not twins, they will never have identical purposes or results.

But how do these distinctions relate to the subject at hand? Wit and humor in design—the playful manipulation of type and image separately or together—though sharing many fundamental attributes of verbal humor, are not encumbered by similar emotional complexities. Unhampered by the numerous light and dark psychological turns endemic to written or spoken humor, graphic design humor's primary agenda is to attract viewer attention and make a client's message memorable. How this is done is indeed varied and fascinating, but sometimes comparatively simple to achieve.

A MESSAGE FROM DR. FREUD Before focusing exclusively on the historical manifestations and contemporary characteristics of wit and humor in design, it is important to explore briefly—and generally—the nature of wit and humor's effects on the funny bone (or their "relation to the subconscious," as Sigmund Freud said in his 1905 famous essay on jokes). Moreover, before we delve into realms exclusively visual and specifically graphic, we should define wit and humor, since the basic definitions are relevant to all media and forms. Rather than putting my faith entirely in Mr. Webster's dictionary definitions, however, I have consulted a few other experts for their opinions. With their help, I will first discuss humor, and then wit.

James Thurber said, "Humor is emotional chaos remembered in tranquility," while Mark Twain wrote, "The secret source of humor is not joy, but sorrow." Cartoonist and author Don Herold tells us, "The nearer humor is to pain, the longer it is apt to last." And journalist Kenneth Bird coined the old chestnut that goes, "Humor is falling downstairs if you do it while in the act of warning your wife not to." Turning to the dictionary, we are told that "humor is a changing (or fluid) state of mind"—which is exactly what one would expect from a cool dictionary definition. So I prefer Groucho Marx, who, though no more precise than Mr. Webster, is much warmer when he says, "There are all kinds of humor. Some is derisive, some sympathetic, and some merely whimsical."

According to these experts, humor is a combination of actions and reactions, often rooted in turmoil. Nevertheless, they all seem to find it

HELVETICA T-SHIRT USED TO PRO-
MOTE ITC GARAMOND TYPE, 1989
DESIGNER: JACK SUMMERFORD
WRITER: JACK SUMMERFORD
CLIENT: SOUTHWESTERN
TYPOGRAPHICS, INC.

either too complicated to define precisely (or perhaps they feel it is unnecessary to do so). In *Enjoyment of Laughter,* a definitive 1936 text on the subject of jokes, Max Eastman says rather nondefinitively that "Humor at its best is a somewhat fluid and transitory element." But even if we could all agree on a universal definition, would this intellectualizing enhance our appreciation of humor? Isn't it true that if we analyze—or vivisect—a joke, verbal or visual, it then loses its specialness and is therefore no longer funny? Humor, after all, relies on the unexpected—a clinical explanation of humor would reduce the element of surprise. Eastman asserts that "a study of the classification of the kinds of humorous experience on the basis of theory as to its nature is a . . . science . . . [but] it is not, to be sure, a vitally important science." Understanding the distinction between good and bad humor, he argues, does not ensure that one's sense of humor or one's ability to tell a joke will improve. Therefore, as unscientific as it may sound, I've concluded that humor is in the genes at birth, and is sparked by the instinct for play that all children have.

Classic humor will always be funny despite the folly of those pedants (like myself) who try to analyze it. For this humor is neither topical nor fashionable but timeless and true. I cannot remember how often I have seen and laughed at the same jokes over and over in my favorite films, such as the Marx Brothers' *Duck Soup* and Woody Allen's *Annie Hall.* Or, for that matter, at the vintage advertisements, like George Lois's 1962 Wolfschmidt's Vodka campaign and Helmut Krone's 1960 Volkswagen "Lemon"

campaign, which are so conceptually astute—and have become so paradigmatic of their genre—that I continue to be awed by their brilliant yet simple humor. Since I hate the old adage, "I don't know what humor is, but I know it when it hits me," I shall give you this explanation of humor by author Howard Brubaker and offer it as my own: "[T]he common denominator of humor is the contact of incongruous ideas. This mixture causes a series of little explosions as in an internal combustion engine."

If humor is like fuel, then wit, said George Herbert, "is at times an unruly engine." As the word phonetically suggests, wit is fast paced—a swift perception, usually of the incongruous. In contrast to a less sophisticated form of humor, like jest, which Sigmund Freud describes as "nonsensical comic relationships made by children or childlike adults for the purpose of pure pleasure," wit is the ability to control incongruous or nonsensical stimuli for purposes of tapping into deeper reservoirs of human experience.

Unlike play, a rather joyful and random activity that is key to all humor, wit involves a greater degree of cleverness and sarcasm. Wit, therefore, runs the risk of being too self-conscious—being witty can be both a gift and curse. For the nineteenth-century critic William Hazlitt, "Wit is the salt of conversation, not the food." Though I fundamentally disagree with the notion that wit is merely seasoning for a greater intellectual feast, I do seriously consider the validity of the following statement, made a few centuries earlier by the philosopher John Lyly in *Anatomy of Wit*: "I have ever thought so superstitiously of wit, that I fear I have committed idolatry against

wisdom." I believe that while some wit has a foothold in wisdom, wit can also be misused and misdirected. Not too long ago, novelist Geoffrey Bocca brilliantly described wit as "a treacherous dart. It is perhaps the only weapon with which it is possible to stab oneself in the back."

EFFORTLESS COMPLEXITY True wit, though volatile, depends on the mastery of various forms of language. The witty writer, for example, is a verbal acrobat whose high-wire antics rely on precision timing and acute understanding. No matter how precarious the death-defying feat, this writer must land perfectly on his or her feet. The great humorous writers are known for crafting figures of speech into vivid mental pictures. As a classic example, let's take the phrase *dog bites man,* which is neither funny nor news. Conversely, *man bites dog* is both news and somewhat funny because it twists the ordinary. But, more to the point, *man bites man* is not only a surprising concept but at once a vividly absurd picture revealing two simultaneous concepts. At the risk of committing *humorcide* through overanalysis, I submit that in this phrase one man is not only physically assaulting the other in a rather annoying and unconventional manner, but that since the word bite also suggests ridicule or criticism, it gives the phrase an additional level of meaning, causing it to be even funnier than its literal content suggests. Another example of such skillful verbal wit comes from Max Eastman, who quotes a young World War I soldier after the latter's first visit to Paris's legendary *Folies Bergere:* "I never saw such sad faces or such gay behinds." In addition

to having the sting of a sound-bite, this is a sage observation conjuring a real-life portrait of the vivacious but overworked sex objects who danced the famous Can Can night after endless night in the Parisian nightclub. What these examples suggest is that the most skillful wit must appear effortless while being loaded with meaning. Even Aesop said something to the effect that "clumsy humor is no joke."

LOW HUMOR/HIGH WIT Graphic wit should be no exception. The best design solutions must appear not only effortless but free from the self-conscious and tired conceits of all belabored humor. Yet if this is true, then why is it that the pun is one of the most significant components of graphic wit and design humor? As the oldest form of humor, the pun is also considered in the world of letters—as in the world—to be the lowest form. There is no kind of false wit that has been ridiculed as much as the pun, said one critic. Yet a pun, the dictionary tells us, is "the humorous use of a word or words which are formed or sound alike but have different meanings, in such a way as to play on two or more of the possible applications; a pun is a play on words." Though the theory is sound, Edgar Allan Poe complained about the practice that "The goodness of the true pun is in the direct ratio of its intolerability." An old English proverb goes, "Who makes a pun will pick a pocket." And who can forget that old grade-school put-down, "*PU* is two-thirds of a pun." Indeed, throughout the ages this venerable form has been so abused that the *New York Times* forbids puns in its headlines unless the word substitution is so inextricably linked to the meaning of the story that the pun is incidental.

However, to answer the question of why puns are necessary in graphic wit and humor, one must understand that the rules that govern verbal language do not translate precisely into visual language. Thus, the *New York Times* has no rules governing visual puns. Graphic designers' canon of usage is different because our means of communication—our language, syntax, and grammar—are different. A picture is worth a thousand words because so much more information can be evoked through one image than in a sentence or paragraph. In visual language, it often is necessary to substitute one image for another, or one symbol for another—not just for purposes of jest, but to enhance meaning. Therefore, the pun—at best a kind of shorthand, at worst a strained contortion—describes graphic symbols used to simplify complex concepts into accessible, often memorable images.

Paul Rand, in *A Designer's Art* (Yale University Press, 1985), says visual puns are the keys to some of his most successful designs, since "they amuse as they inform." The elevation of the pun from jest to graphic communications tool must also be credited to one of Rand's former Yale University students, Eli Kince, whose *Visual Puns in Design* (Watson-Guptill, 1982) argues that a pun is the conveyor of credible visual messages. If the pun is the lowest form of verbal humor, Kince reasons, this may beg the question, "Is graphic humor at the low end of the evolutionary scale?" Kince quotes Charles Lamb saying puns are "a pistol let off at the ear, not a feather to tickle the intellect." Remember too that the best verbal puns are not simple-minded rhymes but truly surprising (even shocking), yet decidedly logical, manipulations of language. So at the risk of sounding hyperbolic, the best visual puns have a similar effect on perception as, say, a right cross to the chin, for the result is indeed staggering. With the logo for *Families* magazine, the late typemaster Herb Lubalin created a rather literal symbol for *family* out of the letters *ili,* resulting in a memorable icon. For the reader or viewer, it was also a rebus, which, when recognized, added another level of appreciation. When a visual pun works—specifically, when two distinct entities merge to form one idea—the effect stimulates thought and sensation.

MEASURING WHAT'S FUNNY The first law of humor that Max Eastman quotes in *Enjoyment of Laughter* is that "things can be funny only when we are in fun." There may be a serious thought or motive lurking underneath our humor. We may be only "half in fun" and still be funny. But when we do not have the spirit of fun at all, when we are, as Eastman warns, "in dead earnest," humor is the thing that is dead. This implies a distinction between fun and funny, an idea dating back to ancient Greek theater (in fact, much of what we call comic can be traced to this source), when irony was first used as a means to teach moral tales. Though the messages were serious, indeed tragic, the means to achieve catharsis were often conveyed through humor—a humor that shed light on the truth.

Groucho Marx's description of diversity in verbal humor, applies as well to graphic wit and humor, but one difference between verbal and design humor is apparent: the latter cannot always be measured by laughter alone. In fact, I doubt that anyone reading or looking at the images in this book would double over from laughter, because that is not the nature of graphic design humor. As a selling tool, graphic design humor might be described as a loss leader—a means to grab attention and lure the customer or client into the store. Humor, then, cannot be too outrageous, lest the purpose be defeated. Even as a political weapon, humor similarly functions to sell a message, sometimes by ridicule, but is often subtle or sardonic, not ripsnortingly funny. At best, humorous design will force a laugh, bring a smile, or cause a double take, which is nothing to be ashamed of. Indeed, like hypnotic suggestion, the goal of graphic wit and design humor is to *subvert* the subconscious and thereby earn a market share of memory. If, for example, Milton Glaser had designed his "I ♥ New York" trademark using an elegant typeface and spelling the word *love,* it would be humorless, and probably unmemorable; instead he created "I ♥ New York," which, although not a sidesplitter, is a witty combination of word and symbol that today is a much-imitated visual device.

Humor is a mnemonic tool—something that helps (or forces) us to recollect. This can be manifest in *wordplay,* like a slogan or jingle, or *picture play,* such as a logo or trademark. An example of the former is the brilliant slogan for the daily newspaper *New York Newsday:* "On Top of the News and Ahead of the Times." In that simple phrase, *Newsday* memorably positions itself as both a superlative newspaper and wor-

thy competitor. On first reading, *On Top of the News* implies breaking its share of news stories, while *Ahead of the Times* implies being progressive but not doggedly fashionable. But it also invokes the claim that *Newsday* is better than the *New York Times* and the *New York Daily News.* An historical example of picture play is a three-panel Dubonnet poster designed by A. M. Cassandre in 1932, which even today is memorable for its playful wit. In his marriage of word and image, Cassandre's comic trade character, the "Dubonnet Man," sits drinking the wine at a café table. In panel one, he is rendered mostly in outline, his partially painted arm outstretched with glass in hand; underneath, the word DUBONNET is rendered half in bold, the rest in outline, focusing the viewer's eye on DUBO. In the second panel, the character is drinking as his outlined body begins to fill with color and detail, and another letter, the N, is now bold, revealing DUBON. And in the last panel a completely rendered character is pouring from a bottle to refill his glass, and the word DUBONNET is completely bold. This brilliant visual "jingle" has multiple levels of meaning: In French, *dubo* means "something liquid," *dubon* means "something good," and Dubonnet is indeed a wonderful wine. The fast cadence of DUBO, DUBON, DUBONNET is appealing for its almost rhythmic syncopation, but there is something else going on here—in addition to the sophisticated verbal and graphic tricks, Cassandre used a more fundamental aspect of humor to achieve the final result, an activity called the play principle.

In *Thoughts on Design,* Paul Rand asserts that play is essential to the practice of all graphic design. Play is a kind of abandon, yet, as we know from small children, play is their work. In the initial stages of a project (and possibly throughout), the designer ostensibly becomes an adult child, allowing attachments to shift capriciously from one plaything to another. In design, however, playthings are type and image, which are really puzzle pieces to be more or less instinctively moved, juxtaposed, and even mangled and distorted until a serendipitous relationship between formal and contextual problems is achieved. Even the most rigidly systematic design solutions are born of play.

"Humor *is* play," said Max Eastman. Though all humor derives from play, play does not always result in humor. The play principle in design involves intuition, and intuition is a switch that starts and stops the play process, controlling when a designer will move from childlike abandon into adultlike premeditation. What we will call design intuition is not, however, a parapsychological force, heavenly gift, or atavistic trait, but rather a mixture of unreasoned and learned knowledge. Indeed, one way to describe design is as equal parts play and intuition, dictated by the requisites of the problem at hand, and play alone cannot be considered design in the formal sense until an overriding intelligence puts the variables into some kind of order. Moreover, though born of play, graphic design is not inherently humorous. Design humor is the deliberate merging of incongruities into some kind of credible communication that is not overshadowed by reason but is nevertheless governed by it. Wit and humor in design occur when play and logic are seamlessly intertwined.

NOT EVERY DESIGNER A HUMORIST

I am not a humorous designer, at least given the standard that the best visual humor is surprising, fresh, and unencumbered by cliché. Indeed, many otherwise very talented graphic designers are unable to translate good verbal senses of humor into visual humor—some have the knack, others do not. This book is repleat with examples of those who do. But even in this compilation, the qualitative range varies. The exemplars are those who invent new forms rather than conforming to tried and true formulae. They might take chances with subjects and themes that have traditionally defied humorous treatment, like annual reports, and they realize that the easy solution is not necessarily the best, and that effective humor is not always an easy solution.

While I will attempt to "deconstruct" the process of wit and humor in design in this book, there are no correct formulae. Do not read it with the idea that this is *Graphic Comedy 101*. For though humor can be explained, it cannot be taught. While certain formal characteristics are common to all humor in design, like exaggerated scale, odd juxtapositions, and ironic relationships, these same traits also apply to "straight" design. To be certain, a big head placed atop a little body does not ensure hilarity, and a piece of nostalgic clip art used in a work does not *a priori* make it funny. Humor in design is an art, not a procedure. With that in mind, this book will not make a serious designer funny, nor a funny designer an even brighter wit; it will, however, examine a range of ideas and forms in the work of others, so that even if we cannot be great graphic humorists, we can appreciate those who are.—*S.H.*

"SOS" poster, 1990   Designers: Susan C. Harp, Douglas G. Harp   Client: Corning Friends of Earth Day

PART ONE

Anatomy of Wit

Dissecting humor can be a perilous activity. Wit and humor are fragile at best, with overanalysis often resulting in witless and humorless conclusions. Therefore, the purpose of this section is not to disassemble witty or humorous design into its component parts, but to explore some fundamental formal and stylistic characteristics common to all types of graphic design, especially those witty and humorous.

PREHISTORIC HUMOR The origins of visual humor might be traceable to the platypus, whose prehistoric ancestor emerged from the slime millions of years ago near what is now northern Australia. This aquatic mammal with beaver body and duckbill face was possibly Mother Nature's attempt at a visual joke. If this seems a cruel assessment, then consider the suggestion that she was playing with random forms, not unlike a designer sketching an initial idea, never intending to end with

THE PLATYPUS.

this design until seriously smitten by the platypus's comic physiognomy. However, it's no joke that prehistoric man applied his humor primarily to animals—the first true graphic wit was probably represented in depictions of animals on the walls of early cave dwellings. Evidence at Lascaux and other caves indicate man's first attempt at interpretative and caricatural art in the form of drawings of local animals.

HOLY HUMOR A brief examination of the roots of contemporary graphic wit and design humor reveals that the basic methods for achieving visual humor have not been radically altered in ages. Early graphic wit can be traced back to ancient Egyptian papyrus drawings showing anthropomorphized animals that were given symbolic guises by renegade social critics, who used them to represent aspects of human folly. However, the earliest of what we shall loosely refer to as graphic design humor originated in early Christian illuminated manuscripts, prayer books, and psalters from around the eighth century. These are the first examples of the primary graphic design ingredient, the letterform, being seamlessly tied to an image. (For an excellent discussion on this subject, read *Letter and Image* by Massin [Van Nostrand Reinhold, 1970].) It is in these odes to *The Word* that scribes made letters from drawings of contorted human bodies as well as zoomorphic cryptograms of animals real, fantastic, and sometimes funny. Some illuminations were serious symbolic interpretations of holy scripture, while others were just grotesque or ridiculous juxtapositions conceived for the scribe's simple pleasure of constructing a fanciful letter.

Dragons and serpents slithered their way

STYLIZED <u>K</u> FROM BERLIN ALPHABET, C. 1400.

into manuscripts during the ninth century, their scales, tails, and tendrils interweaving with the text in sometimes illegible compositions. Likewise, pictures of exotic vegetation and foliage, witty in terms of their placement on the page, began growing like kudzu on other manuscripts of the same period. Eventually, these intricate visual decorations evolved from truly biblical allegories and symbols into nightmarish creatures, including quadrupeds with human heads, two-headed birds or griffins, humans with paws, plants with beaks, and winged cattle—similar to medieval gargoyles, which anticipated nineteenth-century surrealistic imagery. Many of these initials and marginal decorations had no relationship whatsoever to their texts, and it seems that the illuminators (or designers) were not just being comic or playful, but delinquent in their duties. Actually, Massin writes that the scribes and illuminators from different monasteries competed with each other, as if in some obsessively perverse design competition, to see who might achieve the most outrageous visual folly.

In the fourteenth century, a backlash against this trend toward visual farce was initiated by the leading clerics, who established a canon for the proper illumination of sanctified manuscripts. And for a short period, graphic humor was controlled, if not eliminated entirely. With the perfection of woodblock and copperplate engraving around the fifteenth century, letter-

forms once again became comic in theme though rigid in form, in part owing to strictures imposed by the media. Contrasted to earlier outrageous designs, which extended beyond the letterform confines into the page margins and text areas, these subsequent engraved illuminations told an entire visual story within self-contained letter-

GOTHIC COMPOSITION, PROBABLY DESIGNED BY JEAN MIDOLLOW, C. 1830S.

forms known as *casket letters*. These initials prefigured the fancy faces and novelty typography of the late nineteenth century.

EARTHLY HUMOR In the fourteenth century, Romanesque and Gothic architectural styles were mimicked in period letterforms. The former organically wed excessive ornament to function; the latter featured minimal ornament with a purely formal or aesthetic role. With both, however, visual humor of the kind found in architectural decoration was frequently replicated in the letters. During the middle to late Renaissance, the rules of geometry began influencing concepts of beauty, and so governed the infant art of typography, which as one of its tenets rejected overly decorated (and, by extension, humorous) letterforms. Eventually, the Romanesque, Gothic, and later even Baroque modes of decorative lettering became popular in books and other forms of printing, ultimately influencing a style of humorous graphics found centuries later in commercial typography and design.

During the long interval between the sixteenth and nineteenth centuries, technological and commercial advances significantly altered the role of graphics in society from elitist to populist. Hence, graphic humor became more varied. The communications history of the nineteenth century was heavily molded by the confluence of political, social, and technological advancements. This period of both flowering enlightenment and strict repression had a strong impact on visual humor.

In the 1830s, the development of commercial printing methods, particularly lithography, afforded graphic artists new freedoms of expression and fresh outlets for their talents. Lithography offered greater production flexibility, resulting in low-cost printing for increased quan-

tities. And new distribution methods allowed for greater circulation of what was produced. The most fascinating graphic humor at this time, however, was not found in mass periodicals, as one might expect, but rather in a curious medium: children's alphabet primers. Progressive educators determined that rather than forcing the study of language on youngsters who were more inclined to play than learn, the inclusion of comic visual "games" in their lessons, including metamorphosed alphabets and rebuses, would provide essential learning aids while children played. Similar typographic playfulness was, of course, prevalent in adult-oriented literature in the form of surrealistic and comic initial letters.

The most important outlets for expressive, comic, and satiric graphic art during this time were newspapers in France, the most noteworthy of which was the weekly _Le Charivari_, founded

CHARLES PHILIPON'S CARICATURE OF
THE PEAR KING, 1834.

COVER OF <u>LE CHARIVARI</u>, 1835.

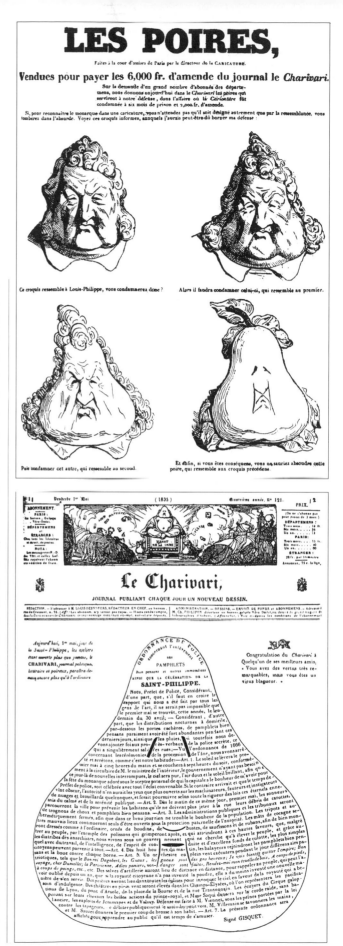

two years after the victors of the July Revolution
of 1830 reinstated a limited monarchy and
appointed citizen King Louis-Philippe to the
throne. *Le Charivari* was the most critically out-
spoken journal in France until its editor, the
writer and cartoonist Charles Philipon, published an image that savagely ridiculed the reign-
ing monarch and became a popular icon of dis-
sent. The image was called *Les Poires* (The Pears),
a four-step transformation of the stout, jowled
king into a plump, overripe pear, which, in addition to being a witty visual metaphor, proved to
be an incendiary insult as well, for le poire in
French slang signifies a simpleton or dope.

Ralph E. Shikes, author of *The Indignant
Eye*, notes that "Many of [Philipon's] fellow
artists, like gleeful delinquents, returned to the
theme again and again." Indeed, The Pear became
so ingrained in the French vernacular that it was
a devastating symbolic blow against authority in
an era when symbols carried great weight—
Louis-Philippe was so threatened by it that he
ordered harsh punitive measures against any cartoonists using the image and eventually decreed
that The Pear (and, not too long afterward, the
entire free press of France) must cease to exist.
But the clever Philipon found a loophole, noting
that the decree *only* prohibited The Pear from
being drawn by an artist's or engraver's hand,
leaving typographical representation unscruti-
nized. In a final act of defiance before the censors
squelched free expression almost entirely,
Philipon published a fiery editorial against cen-
sorship typeset on the cover of *La Charivari* in
the shape of *Les Poires*. This act, though a difficult technical accomplishment, since it was hand-

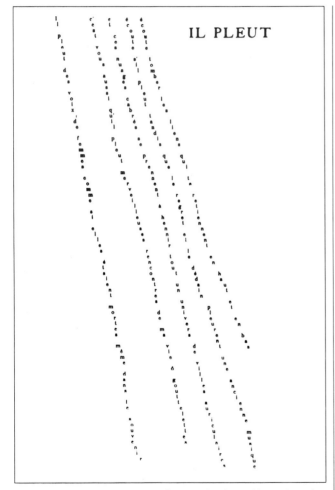

IL PLEUT

set in lead type, was well worth the effort for the consternation it caused officialdom.

Philipon's feat was indeed witty and smart, but it was not, however, a new invention. His typographic manipulation had a history and a name: *figured verse.* It is actually traceable back to long before the advent of moveable type, to when the scribes of Ancient Greece gave concrete form to poetic expression. One of the most famous figured verses in English literature ap-peared in the nineteenth century as "The Mouse's Tail" from *Alice in Wonderland,* in which words form a swirling tail, giving visual emphasis to the character of the mouse. Perhaps the most em-blematic example of this genre is Guillaume Apollinaire's poem, "Il Pleut" (It's Raining), from *Calligrammes, Poemes de la Paix et de la Guerre* (1913–1916), with words that metaphorically fall like rain on a page.

MODERN HUMOR Other Modernist poets and graphic designers also gave voice to words through what one critic has called "noisy" typography. But Appollinaire coined a more poetic term, *calligramme,* to signify a combina-tion of script, design, and thought, "representing the shortest route which can be taken for ex-pressing a thought in material terms, and for forcing the eye to accept a global view of the written word." His revival of this venerable means of expression provided the perfect tool for Modern functionalists, who preferred machine-made imagery (i.e., mechanical and photograph-ic) to hand-made illustration (i.e., realistic draw-ing). Calligrammes and similar typographic con-coctions became the means for progressive artists, writers, and designers to express them-selves economically and functionally with the proper Modern materials. Variations on the cal-ligramme, both witty and profane, were created by members of the Futurist, Constructivist, and Dadaist movements in manifestos expressing the goals of their respective cultural revolutions. Indeed, these documents challenged existing artistic canons even as they questioned conven-tional means of comprehension.

One of the most radical proponents of this new visual language was F. T. Marinetti, the father of Italian Futurism, who invented the *Parole in Liberta* (Words in Freedom), giving sound to typography. As early as 1910, he wrote that to enliven the printed page he would use "three or four inks of different colors on a single page and twenty different typefaces if necessary." His goal was to create a new synthetic means of expression. Moreover, through a visual/verbal assault, he hoped to shock Europe's stagnating

intellects into joining the modern world. However, what he and the other European avant-gardists pioneered as a new language was soon adopted and promulgated by commercial and advertising artists as *style*. While the avant-gardists were challenging and perhaps even having serious fun at the expense of convention, the commercial artists appropriated safe and unthreatening aspects of the Modernist visual vocabulary, establishing new design conventions and making the "far-out" accessible to a mass audience. Indeed, in the hands of commercial artists, calligrammes and other concrete typography were effective means of creating mnemonic devices to ensure product identification. Massin wrote that this method "fuses a visual image and a script and gives a tangible quality to the metaphor. It offers a slogan which is made up of words, a concrete presence and an immediate significance so that its power is reinforced to a remarkable degree."

MODERNE HUMOR The Modern movement rejected antiquated styles. Conversely, the Moderne style—the dominant mode of mass commercial art that ran concurrent with Modernism from the early 1920s to the mid-1930s—enthusiastically embraced them. While the Modernists sought to develop a timeless vocabulary resistant to the erosive effects of fashion, Moderne (or modernistic) designers derived their popular style from a confluence of historical and contemporary influences that was deliberately fashionable and predictably short-lived. Wry, sophisticated humor was key to certain aspects of Modern design, while Moderne design humor

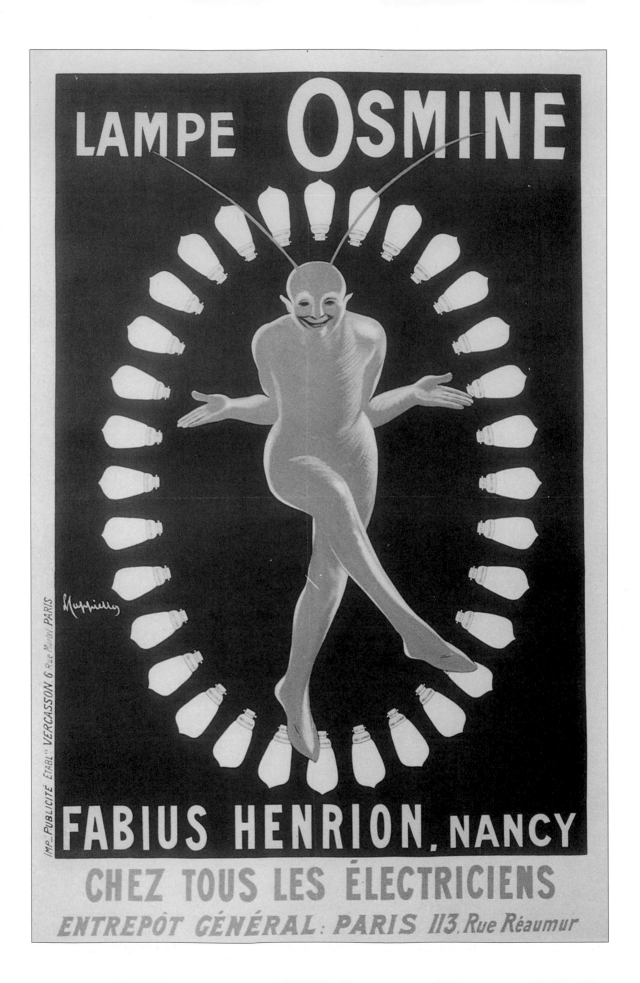

was generally less intellectually rigorous. However, since Moderne design drew its inspiration
from mass culture and was directed at the mass
market, it had to be much more comic in certain
respects, for lightheartedness in advertising and
publicity was a proven commercial lure. Owing
to the limited color palette and type choices of
Modern graphic design, especially as practiced
under the banners of the Bauhaus and the New
Typography, the avant-garde was perceived by
some critics as too austere, humorless, and therefore too off-putting to be successful in the marketplace. Nevertheless, Modernism was accepted
more warmly in Europe than the United States,
where advertising "experts" consistently underestimated public tolerance for things new.

Since Moderne designers did not reject
drawing or painting as viable design tools, and
because their color palette was rich and typographic variations numerous, the range of graphic materials produced under the Modernistic
umbrella was usually quite joyful and witty.
Much modernistic design was illustrative, and
since humor was easier to achieve with illustration than with type alone, Moderne humor must
be viewed as ostensibly pictorial.

Excellent examples of this pictorial mode
include the posters by the Italian artist Leonetto
Cappiello, who was a prolific posterist in France
and Italy during the early twentieth century and
achieved memorable imagery through his comic,
gestural drawings. Cappiello's lettering was bold
and straightforward, with his humor usually
conveyed through a single figure surrealistically
juxtaposed with the object being advertised. An
example of this is the human firefly surrounded

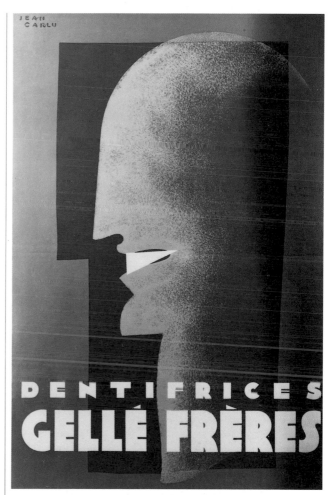

by light bulbs in his brilliant poster for *Lampe
Osmine*. French artist Jean Carlu, another
Moderne master, was not as interested in gestural drawing as was Cappiello but nevertheless had
a pictorial rather than typographic orientation.
His comic images, which advertised a wide range
of quotidian products, were based on a synthesis
of borrowed Cubist forms into cartoonlike signposts. Carlu's poster for *Dentifrices Gellé Frères*
uses stylish lettering to identify the product, but

the focus is on the discordant shapes forming the comic head and shadow. The target is a spotlight on the teeth (which A. Tollmer, a 1930s design critic, called "the graphic dart"). This poster is also clever on another level, for rather than showing a package, as was the convention of the day, Carlu created a semiabstract, comic trademark that was effectively applied to other selling materials.

Carlu was a master but not, however, the originator of this method of pictographic, humorous design. Before him, in the 1910s and 1920s, many German trademark designers, most notably Karl Schulpig, were cleverly playing with stark geometries with the goal of changing logo and trademark imagery from the intricate, heraldic marks of the previous century to simplified and witty graphic pictograms. This change was necessary because business dominance was shifting—small, family-run concerns were increasingly giving way to large, shareholder-owned corporations—and the venerable means of identification were quickly becoming obsolete in this new business culture. Schulpig developed marks and posters that offered a more abstract approach, but never so confounding as to be incomprehensible (like some of today's marks). Many of these images were like puzzles, which, when deciphered, became unforgettable. One exemplary mark designed by John Heartfield for the Malik Verlag, a German socialist publishing company, was a pictogram of a comic robot formed by the sans serif letters *M A L I K*.

CENTER: BOLLE LOGO DESIGNED BY
KARL SCHULPIG, C. 1920.

BOTTOM LEFT, TOP RIGHT: TRADEMARK
SUGGESTIONS IN THE MODERNE STYLE
BY SAMUEL WELO, 1934.

COVER OF THE GERMAN EDITION OF
PUCK, THE AMERICAN COMIC AND
SATIRE JOURNAL, 1881.

COVER OF HARPER'S WEEKLY, 1901,
IN WHICH NO ATTEMPT IS MADE TO
INTEGRATE IMAGE AND TYPE.

COVER OF SATIRE, 1911, SHOWING
UNIFIED DESIGN.

BOTTOM: TRADE CHARACTER FOR
BELL TELEPHONE, BY AN ANONYMOUS
ARTIST, 1934.

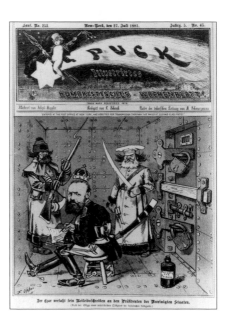

ILLUSTRATION VS. DESIGN

Not all pictorial humor is design humor. While many forms of illustration and cartoon are used in concert with type, only some of these relationships are actually driven by design. Cappiello's imagery was definitely illustrative, but the drawings in his posters were not used to tell a narrative story (which is my simple definition of illustration), but rather as mnemonic symbols. Similarly, Carlu was not making narrative illustration, but rather a pictorial symbology that developed from design requisites.

Shown here are examples of purely humorous illustration on the covers of *Harper's Weekly*,

Satire, *Liberty*, and the *Saturday Evening Post* magazines, in which no attempt is made to unify the typographic elements with the artwork. Each piece of art is a narrative, telling a story by freezing a moment of time into a vignette or tableau. These images may be witty or even satiric, but they are not examples of design humor. Conversely, the artwork and lettering for the cover of *Vanity Fair*, rendered by its art director, M. F. Agha, is seamlessly intertwined, like a miniposter. The intent of the cover is not to tell a story, but to serve as a signpost announcing that this is the Christmas issue of the magazine. And on page 26 are three billboards (c. 1938), in which comic characterizations are in concert with amusing lettering. While these can be considered design humor, each represents a more slapstick approach than, say, the posters by Cappiello, Carlu, or Agha.

POSTWAR HUMOR A schism of varying degrees has existed between illustrator and designer ever since the advent of commercial printing, which allowed the artist to make artwork in a virtual vacuum, ignorant of how the work would be used in a layout. But at no time was the schism more profound than during the post–World War II era, when descendants of the Modern movement in Europe and the United States fervently rejected drawn or painted illustration in favor of more "objective" or "rational" media, such as photography

LASTS—LONGER

WRIGLEY'S SPEARMINT
THE PERFECT GUM

We lock in all its goodness

Snowdrift
FOR
Cake
Biscuit
Pastry
and
Frying

and give you the key

LOWEST COST PER SEASON

SUPER PYRO
ANTI-FREEZE
25¢ QT.

and photomontage. The direct descendants of the Bauhaus developed the Swiss Style, a rather systematic, functional design approach based on a less-is-more philosophy, which was perceived by its critics as totally devoid of humor. Of course, nothing can be so black and white, and while Swiss design is definitely austere, it is not completely humorless. Indeed, Josef Muller Brockman's much-reproduced poster protesting noise pollution is an economical form but an acerbic and bitter-sweet message.

Swiss design reflected the temperament of the Swiss nation during the postwar years, and also perpetuated the stereotype of their squeaky-clean and well-ordered society. But more importantly, Swiss graphic design was a profound influence on designers elsewhere in the industrialized world, who were beginning to administer to the identity needs of the emerging multinational corporations requiring manageable, uniform design systems. In America, however, small pockets of rebellion grew in response to rationalist trends perceived as cold and humorless. Push Pin Studios, founded in 1954 by the illustrators Seymour Chwast, Milton Glaser, Reynold Ruffins, and Edward Sorel, became the most recognized and influential of these rebels. Push Pin was also the progenitor of a new American eclecticism noted for returning illustration back to the design process. Push Pin developed a distinctive, decidedly humorous pictorial vocabulary by reviving and synthesizing historical European graphic styles and American vernacular art, like the comics, into a cacophony of type and imagery. Humor in all forms—from jest to pun to parody—was key to the Push Pin style. And its

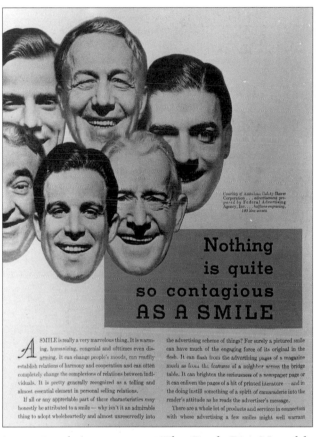

inventive house organ, *The Push Pin Monthly Graphic,* was a proving ground for its various members' graphic humor. Fortunately, Push Pin's clients were primarily in the entertainment, publishing, and culture fields, which tended to prefer to be represented by humor.

LATE MODERN HUMOR Graphic design came of age during the 1950s, when the field was no longer called commercial art, but "art for commerce"—a fine but very significant distinction that implies a higher level of collaboration between artist and business. The leading practi-

ABOVE: WESTINGHOUSE LOGO
DESIGNED BY PAUL RAND, 1960.

LEFT: UNITED PARCEL SERVICE LOGO
DESIGNED BY PAUL RAND, 1961.

BOTTOM LEFT: COVER FOR ANATOMY
FOR INTERIOR DESIGNERS, 1952,
DESIGNED BY ALVIN LUSTIG, USING
ABSTRACTED BODY PARTS IN A LIGHT-
HEARTED MANNER.

BELOW: BRADBURY THOMPSON'S
TYPOGRAPHY MIMICS SOUND IN
WESTVACO INSPIRATIONS, 1948.

tioners were not anonymous craftspersons but respected communicators, some with distinctive personal styles, others with notable philosophies, and a few even holding revolutionary ideas in the tradition of the European avant-gardes. Paul Rand, a very early exponent of progressive design in the United States, made his mark in advertising during the late 1930s through his emphasis on quite playful, visual solutions instead of the ubiquitous copy-driven ads. In the 1950s, he made even more significant inroads into the infant field of corporate communications, combining the best of the Swiss systematic design with his personal passion for play. Rand instinctively imbued his book jackets, posters, and even children's books with wry humor to enhance both eye appeal and meaning, and believed firmly that

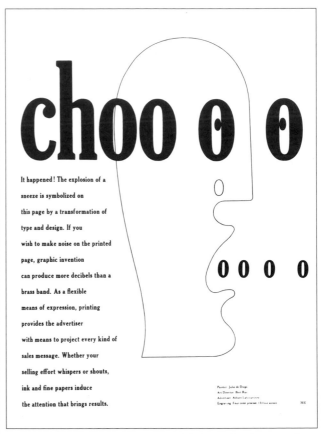

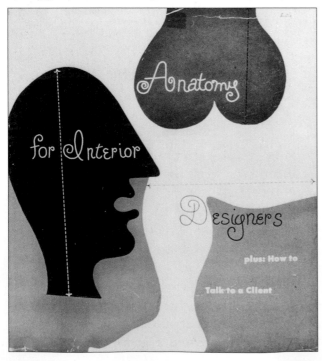

even corporate design could benefit from play. His most visible corporate logos and trademarks are witty visual puns. For example, the logo for Westinghouse, a *W*, is an electrical schematic, while the one for UPS is an heraldic shield with a gift box as a crown.

During the late 1950s, typeplay evolved from the anarchic Dada and Futurist manifestations into more deliberate communications. Bradbury Thompson, who devoted an entire 1949 issue of *Westvaco Inspirations* (the paper company's influential promotional magazine) to the subject of type as metaphor, was himself a

She's got to
go out
to get Woman's Day
the A&P magazine

...and Woman's Day isn't all she buys.
Because Woman's Day's circulation is all single copy sales,
you can be sure of 3,811,000 readers out shopping where your products are sold.

skilled master of this typographic art. Through witty layouts in which type was used to mimic sound, Thompson proved that type was an extraordinarily versatile expressive tool.

If Thompson helped emancipate hot type from the shackles of the chase, Herb Lubalin gave type its many voices, some of them comedic. With the rebus in mind, Lubalin made words and images read together as single entities in compositions that were at once witty and true. But his really important, groundbreaking work came with the advent of the phototypositor, for he experimented with such close settings and contorted juxtapositions that he became known as the "master of smashed type." By tightening, touching, and overlapping letterforms, he forced a radical break from the standards that had governed typesetting for ages. At the same time, he tamed the more anarchic manifestations of the avant-garde into an *au courant* typographic language, at once playful and accessible.

Prefiguring sound-bite mania, but concurrent with television's rise in popularity during the early 1960s, the brightest American advertising art directors, in collaboration with their creative team partners, created a genre of word/image advertising notable for its straightforward design, matter-of-fact image (usually photographic), and sophisticated wit. Influenced by television, the best print campaigns competed successfully with the tube for memorability. Indeed, three campaigns are still unforgettable after almost three decades, because their ideas were so ingenious and the design so innovative that they continue to defy quibble and qualm: George Lois's Wolfschmidt's Vodka campaign, in which tasty fruit and vegetable additives converse smartly with tasteless alcohol; Helmut Krone's Volkswagen campaign, the first time an advertiser revealed its own faults in public; and William Taubman's Levy's Rye Bread campaign, in which various members of New York's ethnic melting pot declared on large subway posters that "You don't have to be Jewish to love Levy's." In addition, Lou Dorfsman, design director for CBS, was writing and designing brilliantly witty advertising during this period. Though well-crafted words are the keys to the success of these ads, memorability is based on the sum of their parts—text, image and typography—as well as on their confident and at times self-effacing humor.

POST-MODERN HUMOR

The term Post-Modern, when applied to graphic design, is an attitude, not a style, associated with the time period from the mid-1970s to the present. Literally, *Post-Modernism* is historiographic nomenclature for the ethic that follows Modernism. Philosophically, it describes a reassessment and revival throughout art and design of historical and vernacular styles and materials formerly rejected by Modernism and outmoded by fashion. In architecture and literature, Post-Modernism, simply stated, is an analytical process of "deconstructing" a particular work in order to discover its formal origins; in graphic design, however, the term is merely a convenient catchall for a broad range of contemporary design applications, none of them directly related to each other by one dominant ethic. Post-Modern graphic design is neither a movement with a moral mission nor a school with shared beliefs, but rather a number of vaguely linked aesthetics. When the history of the period from the mid-1970s to the 1990s is codified, it will include an array of computer, vernacular, historicist, decorative, and informa-

minor shared attributes, the most significant characteristic to emerge from Post-Modernism is a profound sense of play and humor.

The Post-Modern play ethic began during the postpsychedelic era in the early 1970s with the short-lived, youth-inspired design language called Punk. Punk was reheated Dada without the content, and souped-up 1960s pop without the Vietnam War as an anchor for moral indignance. Punk, which began in England as a musical trend and spread as a design style throughout Europe and the United States in publications like *Slash, New York Rocker,* and, predictably, *Punk,*

tional designers who might superficially share similar color preferences or borrow from the same big closet of revivals—some of the design from this period may look like it was cryogenically preserved back in the 1930s, while other pieces will seem to have returned from the twenty-fifth century. But more important than these

M⊕THER

was about kids coming of age—cynical, sarcastic, angry, and anarchic kids. Punk's design humor was acerbic but not necessarily strident, raucous but not really intelligent. It was a slap-and-paste ethic. Formalism be damned, expression was supreme. Punk's jugular humor wore thin, as did the "movement" itself, which quickly lost steam and was assimilated into the mainstream within a few years of its initial surge of energy.

Replacing Punk was New Wave, or what the cartoonist Gary Panter calls "sanitized punk." New Wave took the primitive Punk visual utterances and transformed them into visual language, with syntax and grammar. The vocabulary was comprised of soothing colors, a plethora of geometric dingbats and ornaments, and humorous imagery often borrowed from old commercial-arts manuals. New Wave designers made it possible to apply Punk to mainstream advertising, the same way Moderne designers had borrowed aspects of Cubism for commercial purposes decades earlier.

If Punk contributed anything to the practice of graphic design, it was the idea that somehow everything was possible—rules didn't matter. Of course, not all designers (or clients, for that matter) are comfortable with such freedom, but that

didn't inhibit young designers in the 1980s from experimenting, even if it meant reinventing the wheel. This spirit also encouraged older designers to alter their methods: Wilburn Bonnell veered from the path of orthodox Modernism into more adventuresome realms; Paul Davis turned from his successful, primitive/surrealist illustration style to graphic design influenced by radical history; Rick Valicenti completely rejected the conservative corporate design he was practicing in favor of euphoric typographics underscored by a theretofore nonexistent sense of humor.

If American graphic design came of age in the late 1950s, it was primarily in New York, Chicago and Los Angeles, the three centers of "enlightened" business and design savvy. In the 1980s, graphic design entered middle age by expanding into regions of the United States where designers had never flourished before. Many of these areas developed somewhat indigenous or regional styles owing to the influence of one or two leading stylists and the kinds of businesses being serviced. In San Francisco, Michael Vanderbyl and Michael Manwaring were influenced by contemporary pop culture (including San Francisco's psychedelic legacy), Post-Modern architecture, and the comic furniture of Milan's Memphis group. Sharing common passions, their work was a synthesis of these contemporary ideas into a distinctive vocabulary of lighthearted New Wave forms underscored by serious visual punning. In Dallas, Woody Pirtle, who was influenced by Push Pin Studios, developed an illustrative design method that was founded on visual puns and witty juxtapositions of content. And in Minneapolis, The Duffy Group exemplified Midwest New Wave styling (in a similar manner to the early work of Push Pin Studios) and a new "vernacular" humor using cuts from 1920s and 1930s printer's manuals. Apparently spellbound by that innocent, yet kitschy, period of commercial art, Charles Spencer Anderson created a vocabulary based on silly but curiously compelling stock images, manipulating them ever so slightly and printing them in contemporary colors. Anderson's approach defined a 1980s genre of graphic humor that will be discussed in Chapter Five.

M&Co., a progressive New York firm, also built its early studio personality on a rehabilitation of old printing forms. But unlike Anderson's quite stylized work, M&Co. used vernacular forms in contrast to (and perhaps as a satire of) the overly sophisticated, indeed superficially decorative trends underscoring American graphic communications. Anderson's approach is rooted in the pleasure that results from playing with these anomalous forms, while M&Co. believes that studying vernacular art provides a method for breaking through the clichés that hamper interesting communication and constrict intelligent humor.

Even in the Post-Modern era, where a simple evocation of the past seems enough to make design humorous, not all humor is based on common nostalgic visual cues. Humor's determinants are complex and fluid, and actively resist categorization. Having now explored the various forms graphic wit and design humor have taken since prehistory, the following chapters deliver on this book's intent: how graphic wit and design humor have evolved in America in recent years.

2 PLAY AT WORK

CIVILIZATION & ITS MALCONTENTS

Play is the work of children. Yet children do not merely busy themselves with playthings, but rather learn invaluable lessons and relationships through processes of discovery inherent in their play. In its purest form, play is joy unrefined, free of constraint. Furthermore, play is the fuel of creativity. Romantically speaking, play is primitivism, because it is not derivative of style or fashion. Since primitivism allows for honest expression, and since children are indeed primitive before becoming "civilized," it is no wonder that artists like Paul Klee, Joan Miro, and Saul Steinberg quote children's imagery as a means of expressing their own primal natures. Neither is it surprising that Abstract Expressionist painting has been compared to the work of children, for despite the grandiloquent art historical theories, many abstract artists in the late 1940s attempted to rediscover those realms of play that society had deemed unsuitable for responsible adults. "Play so that you may be serious," advised Aristotle. "Play freely so that your mind is a welcome home for every new discovery," said a sixth grade art teacher.

Play is a noble activity. Yet in addition to noble play, there is also mischievous play. Though the two should not necessarily be mutually exclusive, sometimes they are direct opposites. While noble play is cherished abandon, mischief is synonymous with premeditated irresponsibility. But mischief can also be more intense play—think about Shakespeare's Puck in *A Midsummer Night's Dream,* who may be devilish but not Satanic, for he is the embodiment of eternal youth. An inveterate prankster, Puck is forever disrupting the status quo, not for the simple pleasure of wreaking havoc but rather as a comic reminder that life should be wonderfully spirited not lifelessly constricted. Puck's distant cousin Peter Pan is the prince of pranks, whose entire existence is forever linked to children's imaginations and their unwillingness to grow up. What's wrong with keeping at least some of the attributes of youth alive, asks Oscar Wilde in *The Picture of Dorian Grey:* "Youth smiles without any reason. It is one of its chiefest charms." What some might call mischief is actually just an attempt to sustain youthful vigor. Whatever the rationale, a certain amount of mischief is necessary for the creative process to begin and continue.

Art and design are to a certain extent driven by mischief. Indeed, the world expects it, and expects to complain about it too. If we look at certain art as mischief in the making, then some of the aesthetic blunders and conceptual stupidities of the contemporary East Village art scene are more palatable. Tracing mischief in art history, one might conclude in hindsight that some of the most well-known blunders and folly were brilliantly rightheaded. For example, as a respite from the rigors of his official commissions, Leonardo da Vinci drew distorted, vexing portraits of noble and common people which were considered beyond the ken of his patrons and inconsistent with artistic convention. Likewise, the sculptor Bernini took certain liberties with the visages of Vatican clerics in mildly "charged" portraits that seemed trivial and beneath his talent, given the artistic standards of his era. But both of these masters' "playthings" became the historical basis for the "serious" art of carica-

SEYMOUR CHWAST'S POSTER FOR HIS OWN 1990 SHOW.

ture. Young Renaissance painters in training engaged in harmless mischief when they painted over academic portraits and landscapes with flies and other crawling creatures, as if in a *trompe l'oeil,* rendered in perfect detail. These pranks provided a reference point for subsequent visual satirists who developed a truly critical art. And jumping into the more recent past, during the early 1920s the Dadaists raised artistic mischief to a high art through images that at once ridiculed the church, army, and government of a morally decaying Germany and created a new expressive visual language based on a menu of aesthetically unacceptable forms. The role of mischief is therefore not to be underestimated.

Play is necessary to the design process because unless a designer is working within a rigid design system that prohibits all variants, exploration is an integral part of all initial problem solving. When a new toy called *Colorforms* was introduced in 1930 with its sheets of brightly colored geometric shapes that adhered to a shiny black board without glue or tape, it became a huge commercial success despite the fact that it was neither a talking doll nor a mechanical toy. Children were fascinated by the countless pictorial variations that were possible with a finite number of geometric shapes. Indeed, many adults were hooked on it too, because it allowed for all kinds of random constructions, like a huge doodle. Colorforms is therefore an appropriate metaphor for the early stage of the graphic design process, which is inherently limited yet curiously limitless. The act of playing with Colorforms is a metaphor for designing, since the image potential is wide-ranging—realistic or abstract; witty or serious; traditional or innovative—just like the range of design solutions in the real world. The first Colorforms instruction manual showed some of the possibilities, including abstract pictures, presumably made by children, that were strikingly similar to Russian Suprematist and Dutch Neo-Plasticist Paintings, as well as the more predictable narrative pictures of girls and boys, ships and cars, and so on. (Incidentally, in 1959 Paul Rand redesigned the Colorforms trademark, using the toy's own available shapes, thereby blending abstract and realistic characteristics into one pictogram.)

The creative potential offered by Colorforms is proscribed not by the limited number of pieces, shapes, and colors but by the child's imagination and skill. If the child's mind is boundless, then so is the game; if the child is constrained by certain limits, then the game has its limits too. To a great extent, this same equation defines the practice of graphic design.

LAW AND ORDER As important as play is to problem solving, graphic design is defined by the imposition of certain limitations and rules, usually imposed by the client, vendor, or printer—every designer must work from a brief and conform to a budget. These real-world determinants distinguish a child at play from a graphic designer at work. These constraints, however, must be seen as a distinct advantage. In *A Designer's Art,* Paul Rand notes in his chapter on "Design and the Play Instinct" that while the ultimate success of a designer's work depends on his or her natural talents, the problem in design

education comes from how to arouse curiosity and stimulate creativity. Rand concludes that limitless freedom is counterproductive and not as useful as the imposition of a set of rules against which the designer can push the recognized limits. Total freedom curiously fosters inertia, because without rules, there can be no motivation to *break* rules. By extension, broken rules often (but not always) imply innovative solutions. Without structure, play becomes energy draining rather than intellectually sustaining.

Graphic design play also differs from child's play in terms of results. This may seem obvious or implicit, but distinguishing the two types of play is nevertheless worth repeating: The child's fingerpainting or collage will be adored by a loving parent no matter what it looks like, while a graphic designer's presentation will be intensely scrutinized by the client. From child's play comes randomness; from adult play comes concept. Random imagery is an end in itself, while concept is the basis for a solution, which translates into visual communication. Humor may be born out of randomness, or even chaos, but humorous design solutions as exemplified in this book must be planned and purposeful.

That designers should be endowed with a play instinct is not surprising—otherwise, why would anyone spend days and nights pushing type and pictures around on sheets of paper or computer screens: That design play must be *controlled*, however, is the critical aspect of creativity—anyone can play with visual or graphic elements, but only a graphic designer can make them into meaningful communication. A designer must know when to play and when to stop. A designer must intuit how far play can be pushed before the fruits of instinct need to be mediated by an overriding logic. Play thus becomes the first step in a process that ultimately involves quick decision making, in addition to astute knowledge of and keen expertise with tools and materials.

FUN IS NOT ALWAYS FUNNY While not all play is humorous, play is definitely the first stage in achieving graphic wit and design humor. Unless a designer can literally project his or her mental picture of a humorous idea onto a page or object with perfect fidelity, then playing with graphic elements until the right relationships emerge is indispensible for achieving a humorous result. While there are no surefire formulae governing wit or humor—in fact, the most successful humor, though rooted in intelligence, is usually serendipitous—there exist some accepted formal tools that designers must use to create a nurturing environment for the humorous idea. Some of these devices are obvious (and even clichéd), others are not.

Veteran vaudevillians used to say that performers could ensure laughter if they took pratfalls, accepted pies in the face, insulted "dames," or simply berated their audiences. (Given the dubious success of Andrew Dice Clay, the sexist/antagonist principle is still disappointingly valid.) Circus clowns have a virtual catalog of visual gags and tricks guaranteed to "make 'em roll in da aisles every time." And in *Enjoyment of Laughter,* Max Eastman acts as a self-appointed lawgiver to the would-be joke teller in his "Nine Commandments of Comic Arts":

1. Be interesting.

2. Be unimpassioned.

3. Be effortless.

4. Remember the difference between cracking practical jokes and conveying ludicrous impressions.

5. Be plausible.

6. Be sudden.

7. Be neat.

8. Be right with your timing.

9. Give good measure of serious satisfaction.

Are there equivalencies in the graphic arts? Being neat has never been an important stipulation (neither, for that matter, has legibility), and one might also argue against being too unimpassioned, but some of the other tenets are applicable to graphic design. There are scores of manuals and guides authored by self-styled comedians telling would-be cartoonists and illustrators how to draw funny pictures, and neophyte graphic designers what hilarious novelty typography to use. Printers used to keep reference books with cartoony stock cuts, which any client with a taste for the silly could buy to add the touch of wit to an advertisement or brochure. Without exception, these guides offered a diet of clichés and stereotypes—in fact, reusable printer's cuts were officially called "clichés." Yet smart design humor cannot be achieved by following blueprints of any kind. Play is not a formulaic activity, and mimicry will not ensure a successful result. Perhaps only by example can designers be exposed to what works and what does not. And even then, what works for one design problem might not for another.

With this in mind, the following sections are not intended to bless the reader with an acute prowess in matters witty and humorous, but rather to explore the formal concerns common to all graphic design with an eye to how distortion, juxtaposition, repetition, transformation, scale, and shape are manipulated for witty or humorous ends. The material used as examples ranges from subtle to hilarious, from light-hearted to acerbic.

DISTORTION In this era of couch-potato home-entertainment systems, the great old traveling carnivals, like the ones featured in the classic film noirs *Nightmare Alley* and *Gun Crazy,* with freakish sideshows and other odd attractions, have all but disappeared. But for those who have a lust for bizarre amusements (as well as good clean fun and games), there remain the county agricultural fairs. These annual celebrations of beef and pork on the hoof are probably the last places in America where one can experience real carnival midways and funhouses, and among the last places to experience the wonderful related attractions. One of the classics is the distortion mirror that stretches and expands a reflection as if it were saltwater taffy. Of all the carnival attractions, the distortion mirror is the most inherently funny, because in stretching and contorting the human form, we see ourselves at our most absurd. No wonder distortion is one of the most common elements in visual humor.

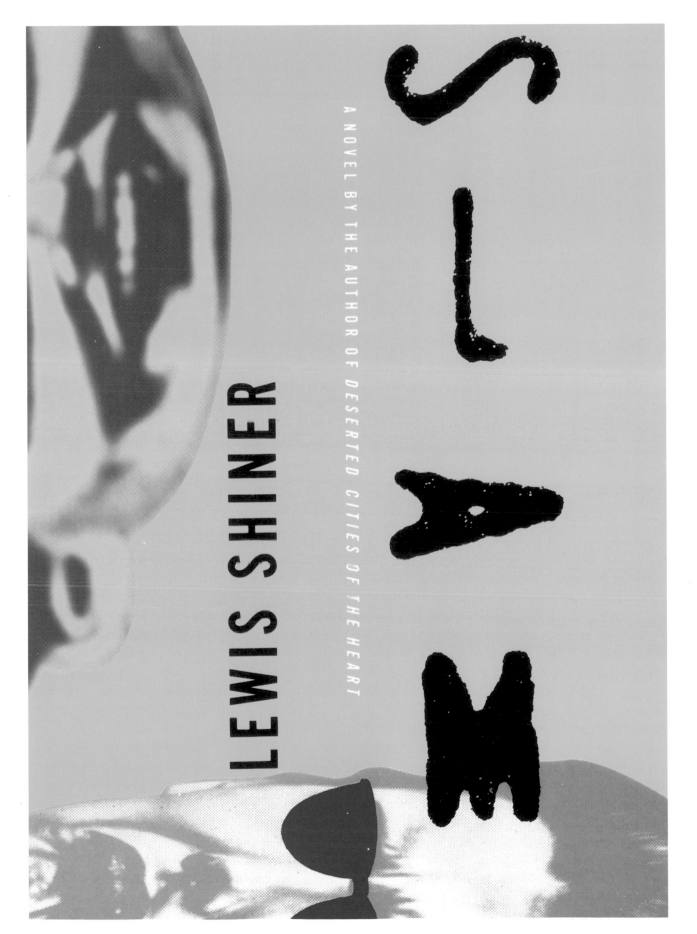

SLAM

LEWIS SHINER

A NOVEL BY THE AUTHOR OF *DESERTED CITIES OF THE HEART*

FRENCH PAPER SWATCHBOOKS, 1989
DESIGNER/ILLUSTRATOR: CHARLES
SPENCER ANDERSON
CLIENT: FRENCH PAPER CO.

RIGHT: 25TH BIRD CALLING
CONTEST POSTER, 1987
ART DIRECTOR/DESIGNER: DAVID
BARTELS, BARTELS AND CARSTENS
ILLUSTRATOR: MARK FREDERICKSON
CLIENT: LEONARD WAXDECK,
PIEDMONT HIGH SCHOOL

Chip Kidd's book jacket for *Slam* does not offer the reader a vivid picture of this novel about a convicted tax evader who lands a job as a caretaker for the estate of a rich old woman who left her fortune to 23 cats (and, given that premise, what could?), but does evoke a sense of the bizarre. By anamorphically distorting stock photographs, cropping, skewing, and printing them in loud colors, Kidd's disembodied heads are reminiscent of the abstract forms made by torn posters on bill postings. And photos are not the only distorted elements of this composition—the title lettering appears to be enlarged well above its original setting, making the typeface unrecognizable as any standard face, which adds to the sense that this design represents many disconnected threads.

If Kidd's distortion produces an abstraction intended to beguile, then Charles Spencer Anderson's comparatively slight distortion of the waiter on the French Paper promotion is intended to personalize an otherwise anonymous rendering borrowed from a 1930s matchbook company sample book. Rather than using it as is, Anderson exaggerates, and thereby caricatures, the stock cut for the purpose of using nostalgia as commentary.

Mark Frederickson's rendering for The 25th Bird Calling Contest is distortion with a vengence. His perfect airbrush painting of the birdcaller, with a Mick Jagger–like mouth opened to extremes that the human jawbone would not tolerate, is the focal point of a piece that is made even more humorous by the idea that this feathered man has just been born, having smashed through a bird's egg.

JUXTAPOSITION All design, graphic or otherwise, is a process of juxtapositioning. A designer must intuitively know where and how

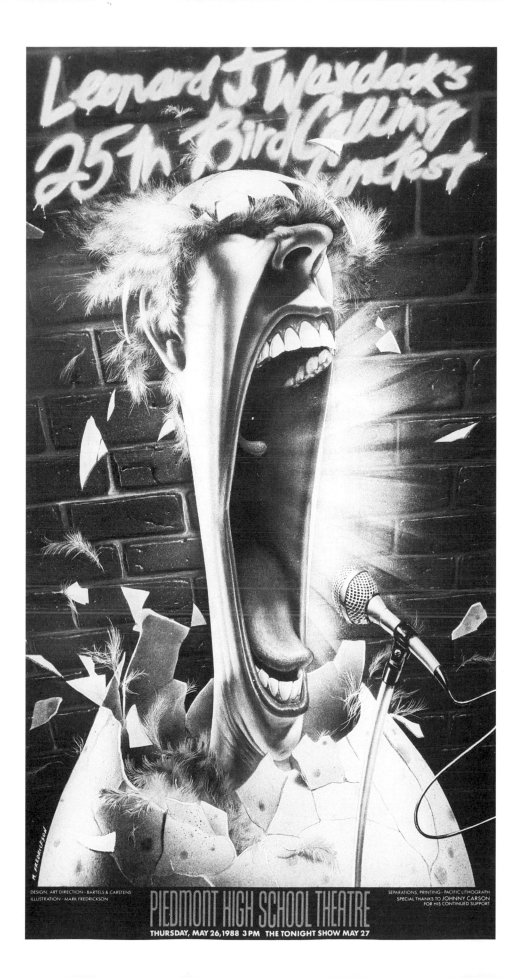

a

insides *outsides*

n

P D P

N

...hat...ee *Open City*... ...en if the picture had been ...ose...resented dead-...an as a stark but moving, ...are...lmost documen...ary story of Italians under ...an-...he German yok...-. Ditto most of the adver- ...gh...ising and public...y for *Paisan*. And then ...ut...*Bitter Rice* came...long and Silvana Man- ...el-gano made exagge...tion in claim... ...re...peal not only unn...essary but...mpossible. ...is *Bitter Rice* was...ctually a...nore than ...the...ually socially c...scious...m about ...nen-omen workers in...ly's ric...fields. To

a nine-days' wonder. It h... quantity and in technical... hasn't turned out an *Open*... who has? Italian films ha... creasingly familiar and in... longer are they a specialized... ...ste. The truck driver, not ju... c...smack his lips over the... c...rms of Gina Lollobrigida... c...nics Caesar and Coca can satirize Italian f...ms to their audience of millions with-

...en th... ...er ...ly ...wea... ...young... ...girdle hom... ...o the student of s... ...havior, th...ignifies neither mass... nor a breakdown of our morality...

LEFT: AIGA "INSIDES/OUTSIDES"
SHOW POSTER, 1990
DESIGNER: RICHARD TURTLETAUB
CLIENT: AMERICAN INSTITUTE OF
GRAPHIC ARTS

"SCREAM" FLYER, 1988
ART DIRECTOR: TOM BONAURO
DESIGNER/ILLUSTRATOR: REX RAY
CLIENT: CENTER

P. INKS BROCHURE, 1989
ART DIRECTOR/DESIGNER:
TOM BONAURO
CLIENT: P. INKS L.A.

to place the operative elements to produce the optimum result. This involves juxtaposing harmonious or discordant images, objects, and letterforms, with no steadfast rules so long as the result is effective. For a massive antinuclear rally held in New York City in 1982, Roger Black designed a simple placard, which said *NO!* in foot-high gothic capitals sitting atop a photo/silk screen of a freshly exploded atomic mushroom cloud. The meaning of this juxtaposition is clear: no more nuclear tests, and *never* a nuclear war. This is not a funny image per se; it is, however, at once a good example of graphic shorthand, and how juxtapositioning works.

The placard is also a kind of rebus, which is a visual puzzle consisting of pictures of objects, signs, and letters, which, when read together, reveal a sentence, phrase, or message. Much graphic humor turns on the ability of the viewer to decipher, read, and understand a graphic message like Black's "NO!" or Tom Bonauro's somewhat more enigmatic "Scream," for an art exhibition in which he and other like-minded thinkers took part. In this picture puzzle, Bonauro juxtaposed a ghosted photograph of a screaming man, a parodic version of Munch's *The Scream* without the screaming figure, and the word *SCREAM* in condensed sans serif type. The game humorously tests the viewer's perceptual ability to fill in the missing piece of the Munch icon. Bonauro extends the boundary of the rebus even further in his brochure for P. Inks. L.A., a rather odd, yet mnemonic, name for a color transfer service. Though the symbolism is ambiguous, the juxtaposition of the logo dropped out of a stark black

UNIVERSAL RHYTHM RECORD
JACKET, 1979
DESIGNER: PAULA SCHER
ILLUSTRATOR: DAVID WILCOX
CLIENT: CBS RECORDS

"EAT" POSTER, 1968
DESIGNER/ILLUSTRATOR:
TOMI UNGERER
CLIENT: SELF

METROPOLIS COVER, 1987
ART DIRECTOR/DESIGNER:
HELENE SILVERMAN
CLIENT: METROPOLIS

band next to an enlarged, halftoned 1950s stock photograph printed in blue, with a smaller iconic cut of shaking hands in the foreground, wittily implies that not only does this firm work efficiently with its clients but that it has a sense of humor and therefore pride in what it does. Are we reading too much into this? Perhaps, but such is the demand of Post-Modern design humor.

Given the Post-Modern sensibility, Richard Turtletaub's poster for the AIGA's "Insides/Outsides" show borrows disparate visual references, to create a somewhat surreal rebus, with symbols that suggest the title (and focus) of this show concerned with complete publication design. The detail of a naked Venus cleverly fits into a quadrant of the fully clothed model (a 1940s stock shot), rather obviously underscoring the insides/outsides theme. A similar effect is achieved by the cross-section of the nautilus shell, the empty picture frame, and the x-ray of a man's head. Although other references in the poster are more obscure, the overall rebuslike effect is quite successful at conveying the message.

On a more obvious footing, juxtaposition works to enhance visual impact as well as meaning in Paula Scher's design for the cover of *Universal Rhythm*. Here illustrator David Wilcox painted over a dozen stylized men's and women's shoes lined up in a row. The shoes are charming by themselves as stationary objects. But as symbols in a row fading toward the horizon they vividly suggest the concept of universality—and when the music begins and the toes start tapping, rhythm, too.

Political propaganda must not be too obscure, since the goal is to communicate a message immediately and without ambiguity. In his 1968 anti–Vietnam War poster, Tomi Ungerer juxtaposed three elements in a no-frills, surrealistic composition requiring little interpretation. The idea that a Vietnamese is being forced to ingest Miss Liberty (a symbol of American imperialism) is a powerful indictment rendered in Ungerer's satiric line.

Collage is one technical means of achieving interesting juxtapositions, as Altman and Manley's shopping bag for Glendale Galleria, Ivan Chermayeff's poster for "New York and The Arts: A Cultural Affair," and Helene Silverman's cover for *Metropolis* magazine exemplify. But in each case, juxtaposition is just one graphic tool among others (including scale change, mixed media, historical referencing, and typeplay, each of which will be discussed in subsequent sections), bringing the incongruous together as one striking image.

"New York Is Museums" poster, 1989
DESIGNER: IVAN CHERMAYEFF
CLIENT: NEW YORK CITY
DEPARTMENT OF CULTURAL AFFAIRS

GLENDALE GALLERIA SHOPPING BAG, 1990
CREATIVE DIRECTORS: BOB MANLEY,
ALTMAN MANLEY
ART DIRECTOR: BRENT CROXTON
DESIGNERS: BRENT CROXTON,
MELINDA MANISCALCO
CLIENT: GLENDALE GALLERIA

REPETITION Joseph Goebbels, the infamous Nazi Minister of Propaganda, asserted that if a lie is told enough times, it becomes true—repetition generates credibility. While only the most simplistic parallel is intended here, many visual artists believe that if something is repeated enough times, it becomes interesting—even funny. Andy Warhol applied this premise to his series of Campbell's Soup Can paintings, and took it to a painfully boring extreme with his experimental films in which one scene (the Empire State Building, for example) was repeated and maintained over and over for hours. Like any aspect of art, repetition only works when the idea or object being repeated is inherently interesting or funny; repetition for its own sake, as an end in itself, is a hit-or-miss proposition.

See The Great Oils At The Memphis Brooks Museum.

Return to a time when artists worked in Brylcreem. See Memphis 1948-1958, an exhibition of postwar photography, art, and popular culture at Memphis Brooks until January 11. Museum hours are Monday through Friday 10-5, and Sunday from 1-5. Open an IRA, CD, Premier Visa or All-in-One Account at First Tennessee and get two free tickets to the show or a commemorative poster when you bring in this ad. FIRST TENNESSEE

David Wilcox's painting of mating rabbits for Paula Scher's record album design of Eric Gale's *Multiplication* is a clever but obvious play off the title. Dean Hanson's decidedly witty use of repeating "greaser" hairdos in conjunction with the headline "See The Great Oils At The Memphis Brooks Museum" is surprising as a bank advertisement but effective nonetheless. But repetition at its most hilarious is exemplified by the *New York Newsday* cover published on the day after former Philippines First Lady Imelda Marcos was acquitted of fraud and theft charges. Among Mrs. Marcos's alleged crimes, she was accused of buying countless pairs of shoes with squandered taxpayers' money, and throughout her four-week trial, *Newsday* had accompanied its courtroom coverage with daily photographs of her footwear, captioned as "the shoe of the day." This device, amusing on its own terms, became even better when *Newsday* delivered its punchline, having obviously planned for the day when Mrs. Marcos would *walk* away from court a free woman. (And what did they have planned in the event of her conviction? "Go Directly to Jail"?)

New York Newsday
EDITION

TUESDAY, JULY 3, 1990 • 25 CENTS

Imelda Walks

Marcos, Khashoggi Acquitted / Pages 4-6

BELOW: AIGA POSTER, 1989
DESIGNERS: CLIFFORD STOLTZE,
RICK STERMOLE
PHOTOGRAPHER: STUART DARSCH
CLIENT: AIGA/BOSTON

RIGHT: COAST TO COAST DIVIDER
PAGE, 1990
DESIGNER: PAULA SCHER
CLIENT: THE L.A. WORKBOOK

than any of the other characteristics in this chapter. Remember the film the *Incredible Shrinking Man?* It played off the absurd notion that someone could be reduced to microscopic size in an otherwise normal world, smartly depicting our fears of helplessness and dread of being symbolically small in our own worlds. More recently, *Honey, I Shrunk the Kids* dealt even more farcically with the same subject. Size change has symbolic impact that, as many very short people know all too well, would take a psychologist to explain. So suffice it to say that scale change is also an important design tool, one that if not always funny, certainly contributes to memorability.

Nineteenth-century caricaturists began the convention of using big heads on little bodies as a means of exaggerating facial features and rendering their subjects helpless—like dolls—in their artistic space. Similarly, cartoonists often increase the size of a subject in relation to nature (e.g., a mammoth body menacing the comparatively tiny and hapless planet earth) as a means of showing empowerment and/or a great threat. Clifford Stoltze and Rick Stermole's design for the AIGA/Boston's New Lecture Series 1989 comically suggests the advent of a design new wave, using a huge silhouetted female head, cropped just above the nose, looming over a powerless, Lilliputian male figure. In a similarly powerful composition, Paula Scher's design for *Coast to Coast* uses a close crop of a giant woman towering over "tiny" World War II planes flying in formation across her body. The anomalous scale relationship here suggests many absurd possibilities.

SCALE Laurel and Hardy and Abbott and Costello are today remembered as much for their emblematic physiques as for a few classic comedy routines. Even if who's who is a blur, the image of fat and thin, short and tall is branded in our memories. These comedians were indeed funny for their slapstick antics, but their humor was definitely enhanced by their looks, with their relative scale changes as the keys. Scale change has a greater effect on our consciousness

Not as menacing, but just as odd, Weiden and Kennedy's ad for Nike's Air Jordan uses scale change to bring home the message that "Michael Jordan has overcome the acceleration of gravity by the application of his muscle power in the vertical plane, thus producing a low altitude earth orbit." Indeed, he is seen flying over a lilliputian Spike Lee and the scientist who presumably made the physics-laden statement, their mouths hung open in disbelief. For added graphic power, they are positioned on top of a miniature photograph of an even more lilliputian planet earth.

Two sunny-side up eggs filling the front and back of a Paula Scher record cover design proves that even a mundane object can be a witty solution when enlarged

beyond expected proportions. Similarly, Rod Dyer and Harriet Baba's cover for *Close Cover Before Striking,* a book of matchbook cover art, magnifies the basically tiny matchbook ten times for an impressive display. Playing with two scale changes, Chip Kidd's extreme reduction of a disembodied head precariously floating in space under a portion of a much larger *Q* on the cover of the *Quarterly* 14 makes the letter seem much more menacing than a mere letter should be.

Anthony Russell uses scale as a humorous conceit on the birth announcement for his son, Daniel, which reminds us that for reasons of cuteness and accessibility, we are predisposed to anything lilliputian or miniature—babies, kittens, and so on. Conve-

TOP LEFT: <u>WEST</u> MAGAZINE COVER, 1969
ART DIRECTOR/DESIGNER: MIKE SALISBURY
CLIENT: LOS ANGELES TIMES

TOP CENTER: "Q 14" <u>QUARTERLY</u>
COVER, 1990
ART DIRECTOR: SUSAN MITCHELL
DESIGNER/PHOTOGRAPHER: CHIP KIDD
CLIENT: VINTAGE BOOKS, RANDOM HOUSE

TOP RIGHT: <u>METROPOLIS</u> COVER, 1988
ART DIRECTOR/DESIGNER: HELENE SILVERMAN
CLIENT: <u>METROPOLIS</u>

BOTTOM: <u>SUNNY SIDE UP</u> RECORD
JACKET, 1978
ART DIRECTOR/DESIGNER: PAULA SCHER
PHOTOGRAPHER: JOHN PAUL ENDRESS
CLIENT: CBS RECORDS

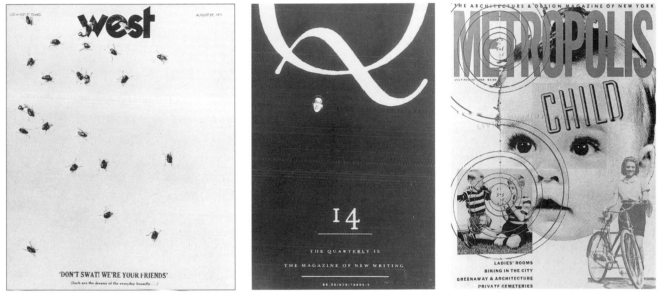

niently, Russell's new baby was exactly the size of a paper merchant's remnant on which the new father printed "Daniel Russell" in foot-wide Pistilli Roman letters, underscored by an arrow spanning the name and a caption, "actual size." To accentuate the joke, a miniature photo of the newborn appears on the bottom of the announcement. A baby is also the focal point for a *Metropolis* cover designed by Helene Silverman, for an issue devoted to designing for children. Here a cute (though disembodied) baby's head is enlarged disproportionately to the other elements of the page. As children themselves have a way of doing, this baby puss serves as a real attention grabber.

Common to these pieces is the technique called *silhouetting*. Indeed, for a scale change to be truly shocking or meaningful in two-dimensional space, it is not enough simply to enlarge or reduce a rectangular image, since the mind is prepared to perceive photographs as big or small; to be credible (or *in*credible, as the case may be), the scale change must appear extraordinary, an impression best accomplished by isolating the form from its surrounding environment by silhouetting.

But not all scale changes are radical enlargements or reductions. Mike Salisbury's cover for *West* magazine has life-size houseflies crawling over the masthead on an otherwise empty page. In addition to the surprise of seeing these pests on a magazine cover, the intuitive given that the shape of a magazine cover defines its own space makes the flies, though not actually exaggerated one way or the other, appear bigger than life.

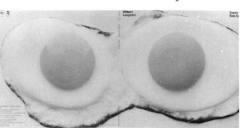

DSVC CALL FOR ENTRIES, 1989
ART DIRECTOR: RON SULLIVAN—
SULLIVAN/PERKINS
DESIGNER/ILLUSTRATOR: JOHN FLAMING
WRITER: MARK PERKINS
CLIENT: THE DALLAS SOCIETY OF
VISUAL COMMUNICATIONS

CARDINAL NUMBERS BOOK JACKET, 1986
ART DIRECTOR: SARA EISENMAN
DESIGNER: MARC J. COHEN
PHOTOGRAPHER: KEN SKALSKI
CLIENT: ALFRED A. KNOPF INC.

TRANSFORMATION The alchemists of old were convinced they could transform lead into gold—a good trick if you can do it—and so were authorized by their noble patrons to spare no expense in the attempt. Given more earthly powers wed to stricter budgetary constraints, today's graphic designers are usually asked to make sow's ears into silk purses. Actually, the alchemists had the easier task—while designers are often called upon to do magic, the reality of how this is achieved is not as simple as having Merlin snap

his fingers, and *presto,* a frog's a prince!—the process is a little more labor-intensive.

We have already discussed distortion, juxtaposition, repetition, and scale change as keys leading to humorous design. But the magic comes when the designer using these tools achieves some kind of transformation by taking the ordinary and making it extraordinary. Actually, like the most effective graphic wit, the best ideas seem effortless—and to a certain extent obvious.

Woody Pirtle transformed the most commonplace household tool, the ordinary

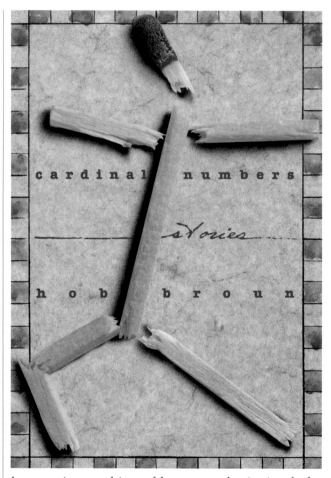

broom, into a thing of beauty and wit simply by painting a score of them with odd colors and shapes, photographing them together, and publishing the results as a long, narrow brochure. A poster for Washington Illustration metamorphoses the typical artist's palette into the shape of Washington, D.C. Bart Crosby put a shirt, tie, suspenders, and horn-rims on a telephone receiver and *presto,* the perfect cover for the Goldman Sachs Funds Group's *Smart Phone Users Guide.* And Drew Hodges saw that the otherwise blocky

"BROOMSHTICK" BROCHURE, 1987
DESIGNER: WOODY PIRTLE
PHOTOGRAPHER: JIM OLVERA
CLIENT: HERITAGE PRESS

PAUL DAVIS SHOW POSTER, 1990
CREATIVE DIRECTOR: SILAS H. RHODES
DESIGNER/ILLUSTRATOR: PAUL DAVIS
CLIENT: THE SCHOOL OF VISUAL ARTS
MUSEUM

MASCOT FOR JEDERMANN SEIN
EIGNER FUSSBALL (EVERY MAN HIS
OWN FOOTBALL); PHOTOMONTAGE BY
JOHN HEARTFIELD, 1919.

MTV logo could be made into a pool table to make a not so obvious but original concoction.

The analogy to magic is particularly apt these days. Comic transformation of inanimate objects into human forms and of human forms into inanimate objects can be attained by a few flips of the computer mouse, the accessibility of which has prompted many designers to play with interesting forms. But this kind of transformation is not necessarily new. One of the earliest "public" uses of photomontage as transforma-

tion tool was achieved by John Heartfield with the little mascot for the Dada journal *Jedermann Sein Eigner Fussball* (Every Man His Own

Football), in which a football man tips his hat to the reader. Decades later, Henry Wolf made a similarly witty manipulation on the cover of *Show* magazine for a story on William Shakespeare. More recently, and without the ben-

MODERNAGE ADVERTISING
CAMPAIGN, 1990
ART DIRECTOR: RICK BIEDEL,
BONNELL DESIGN ASSOCIATES
DESIGNER: RICK BIEDEL
PHOTOGRAPHER: DON PENNY
CLIENT: MODERNAGE

BOTTOM LEFT: "NEVER TOO BIG
FOR OUR BRIDGES" FLIER, 1989
ART DIRECTOR/DESIGNER:
DOROTHY MARSCHALL
ILLUSTRATOR: JAMIE HOGAN
CLIENT: SAN FRANCISCO FOCUS

BOTTOM RIGHT: INNER TUBE BOOK
COVER, 1984
ART DIRECTOR: SARA EISENMAN
DESIGNER: MARC J. COHEN
CLIENT: ALFRED A. KNOPF INC.

FACING PAGE, CENTER LEFT: HAIR
POSTER, 1988
DESIGNER: LINDA SHANKWEILER,
SHANKWEILER SEALY DESIGN
CLIENT: PERFORMANCE STUDIO OF
NEW HAVEN

MTV LOGO, 1989
DESIGNER: DREW HODGES,
SPOT DESIGN
CLIENT: MTV NETWORKS

BOTTOM LEFT: SHOW COVER, 1974
ART DIRECTOR/DESIGNER:
HENRY WOLF
CLIENT: SHOW MAGAZINE

BOTTOM RIGHT: SMART PHONE USERS
GUIDE COVER, 1987
ART DIRECTOR: BART CROSBY
DESIGNER: CARL WHOLT

BOTTOM CENTER: WASHINGTON
ILLUSTRATION COMPETITION
POSTER, 1985
ART DIRECTOR/ILLUSTRATOR:
BURKEY BELSER
DESIGNER: BURKEY BELSER INC.,
CHRISTINE SMITH, MARTY ITTNER
PHOTOGRAPHER: RON JACITZ
CLIENT: ART DIRECTORS CLUB OF
METROPOLITAN WASHINGTON

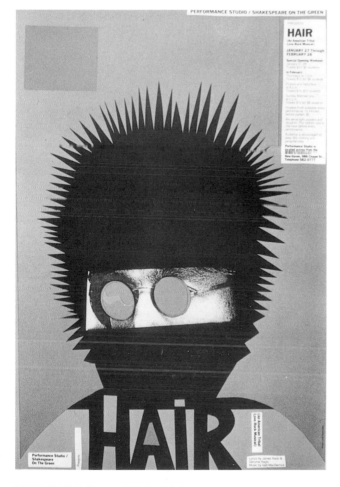

efit of the computer, Rick Biedel transformed furniture into "figureheads" in his sprightly campaign for Modernage, a retro furniture store. Employing a three-dimensional collage approach, Paul Davis conjured up the metamorphic artist from an amalgam of found materials. And using two-dimensional collage, Jamie Hogan illustrated an advertising flier for San Francisco Focus with a figure made from bridges and assorted cultural ephemera.

Among the most common forms of design transformation is making faces from objects. Mark Cohen employed television dials to make a face on the cover of *Inner Tube*, while Sullivan/Perkins blended drawing and television elements together for a face on the call for entries for the Dallas Society of Visual Communicators. And Linda Shankweiler transformed an abstact design into a head for the musical *Hair*.

Whether used together or separately, these formal design elements can result in amusing images. The next section will show how these tools can contribute more cerebral solutions.

3 PUNS & THE LANGUAGE OF GRAPHIC WIT

VISUAL PUNS Not all graphic wit and design humor falls under the umbrella of the visual pun, but an overwhelming majority of what is good in this book, even though it appears in other chapters for formal or aesthetic reasons, can be called puns, because the visual pun is an image with two or more concurrent meanings that when combined yield a single message. The visual pun forces a viewer to perceive an idea on more than one conceptual level. However, if there is no idea, there is no pun.

Not all puns are humorous in the strictest sense. In *Visual Puns in Design,* Eli Kince states that puns have a "humorous effect" and an "analytical effect." The pun is humorous when a certain cleverness and surprise is created. "That mental jolt creates a humorous 'spark,' which releases tension in the form of a smile or a laugh," he says. The pun is analytical when "symbols used in witty and apt ways are appreciated intellectually more than emotionally." As in language, a pun may be a funny joke, a stimulating intellectual synopsis, or, in certain cases, a real stinker. At the risk of sounding repetitious, puns are best when effortless, not strained. The problem with a bad visual pun is, of course, obvious: While a bad verbal pun dissipates in thin air, its visual counterpart is more permanent. The range of puns here is qualitatively varied, but the real stinkers have been eschewed.

LITERAL PUNS The literal pun conveys a message without ambiguity. While this implies the absence of humor, such is not the case. These examples show the various media through which literal puns are communicated, including object,

illustration, photograph, and pictogram. The first example of a three-dimensional object also evidences that some humor is exploitive, if not sexist—this French curve by an anonymous designer is a literal pun because the idea of making a woman into one of these curvilinear drafting templates is a direct substitution of the original meaning. This version shows a curvaceous woman cut from the same fluorescent plastic as real French curves. In Milton Glaser's Olympic

by the number *10*, thus punning on the event and its cycle. Michael McGinn's logo for a department store security agency combines two literal images—a padlock and shopping bag—into one economical mark, while Chiat Day Mojo's NYNEX advertisements use torn-paper puns in the shapes of objects to play off the various Yellow Pages entries. And finally, Seymour Chwast's two posters announcing exhibitions of his work evidence a keen ability to make effortless visual puns. The poster for his Cooper Union retrospective

shows his head twisted back (in a play on the word *retrospective,* which literally means to look back), looking at a lion through the various symbolic filters an artist uses. In the poster for another exhibition (see page 35), Chwast's face is completely empty save for his emblematic pipe, from which a wafting plume of smoke becomes a pun on the map of Brazil, where his show will take place.

SEYMOUR CHWAST RETROSPECTIVE
THE COOPER UNION 3RD AVE & 7TH ST NYC NOV 21 - DEC 12 1986

poster, he takes apart the Olympic logo and the result is a ring toss. Glaser throws the rings onto a Greek column, which without an iota of ambiguity conveys the context of Greek games. Willie Baronet's design for a reunion announcement is a three-tiered message: First, the word *reunion* is constructed out of classic yearbook pictures, indicating that this is not just any old congress, but an annual high school event; moreover, this is not just any reunion, either, but the tenth; and coincidentally, the *i* and *o* are easily substituted

SUGGESTIVE PUNS The suggestive pun is made by combining two or more unrelated or disparate references, sometimes as a substitution for a more literal reference, conveying two or more meanings.

Woody Pirtle's announcement for a lecture in Iowa, shown at right, combines a drawing of the Chrysler Building as a corn cob in a shuck. The suggestion is clear that a city boy has arrived in the country. For UCLA's 1989 Summer Sessions, Pirtle also fabricated a

BELOW: NYNEX YELLOW PAGES
ADVERTISING CAMPAIGN, 1989
AGENCY: CHIAT DAY, N.Y.
PHOTOGRAPHER: MARK WEISS
ART DIRECTOR: MARTY WEISS
COPYWRITER: ROBIN RAJ
CLIENT: NYNEX INFORMATION
RESOURCES CO.
(PRINTED BY PERMISSION OF NYNEX
INFORMATION RESOURCES CO. ©1989)

BOTTOM RIGHT: "MAKING OUR MARK"
EXHIBITION POSTER, 1985
ART DIRECTOR/DESIGNER/
COPYWRITER: CHRIS HILL
PHOTOGRAPHY: GARY FAYE
CLIENT: SOUTHWEST TEXAS STATE U.

AIDS AWARENESS DAY POSTCARD, 1989
DESIGNERS: SUSAN C. HARP, DOUGLAS
G. HARP, HARP & COMPANY
CLIENT: INSTITUTE FOR HUMAN
SERVICES, CORNING, NY
© 1989 DOUGLAS G. HARP

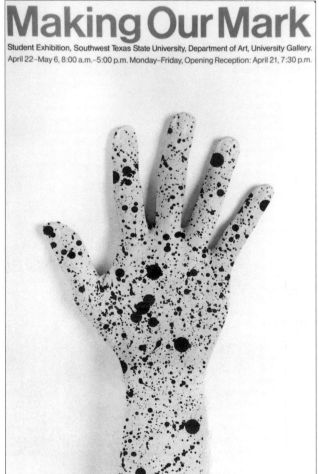

palm tree out of books to suggest not only academics but the tropical southern California clime. Douglas Harp combined the acronym *AIDS* with an hourglass, suggesting that time is running out for victims of this tragic disease. And Rob Boezewinkel suggests that cigarettes are killers in a seamless transformation in which the "cancer stick" turns into a gun.

VERBAL/VISUAL PUNS These are visualizations of aphorisms, sayings, and phrases that are so much a part of our vernacular that the pun is only understandable in that context. For example, "the better mousetrap" is wittily illustrated in Bart Crosby's poster for IDSA's Industrial Design Excellence Awards. *Heat Wave* is represented by a melting record in Robert Grossman's illustration of Paula Scher's record of the same title. "Making Our Mark" is humorously handled in Chris Hill's splattering of the human hand. On page 12, the O in *SOS*, the international distress warning, is replaced by a globe illustrated by Douglas Harp. "Performing

live" is illustrated by Woody Pirtle, who sends a Woody Wagon jumping through a hoop (which is also a double entendre on the aphorism "jumping through hoops," suggesting that Pirtle will be forced to do difficult acts of great skill). Finally, Carin Goldberg's cover for the album *Bread Alone* is a pun on the title with a slight twist, for it shows that indeed, man cannot live on bread alone, but needs a touch of champagne to wash it down.

CLOCKWISE FROM TOP LEFT:

HEAT WAVE RECORD JACKET, 1977
ART DIRECTOR/DESIGNER: PAULA SCHER
ILLUSTRATOR: ROBERT GROSSMAN
CLIENT: CBS RECORDS

AMERICAN CANCER SOCIETY POSTER, 1989
ART DIRECTOR: ROB BOEZEWINKEL
PHOTOGRAPHER: NICK KOUDIS
CLIENT: I. RIMER

"MOUSETRAP" POSTER, 1981
ART DIRECTOR/DESIGNER: BART CROSBY
PHOTOGRAPHER: GEORG BOSEK
CLIENT: INDUSTRIAL DESIGNERS SOCIETY
OF AMERICA

BREAD ALONE RECORD JACKET, 1980
ART DIRECTOR/DESIGNER: CARIN
GOLDBERG
PHOTOGRAPHER: MICHAEL DAKOTA
CLIENT: CBS RECORDS

"PERFORMING LIVE" POSTER, 1990
DESIGNER/ILLUSTRATOR: WOODY PIRTLE
CLIENT: RINGLING SCHOOL OF ART AND
DESIGN

"PALM TREE" SUMMER SESSIONS
POSTER, 1989
DESIGNER: WOODY PIRTLE,
PENNY ROWLAND
PHOTOGRAPHER: BILL WHITEHURST
CLIENT: UNIVERSITY OF CALIFORNIA,
LOS ANGELES

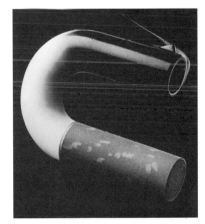

THE IMAGES ON THE FOLLOWING
PAGES, INCLUDING LOGOS, TRADE-
MARKS, POSTERS, AND ADVERTISE-
MENTS, REPRESENT A RANGE OF
LITERAL, SUGGESTIVE, AND
VERBAL/VISUAL PUNS.

THE 1989 LOGO FOR THE PILLAR
CORPORATION, A SOFTWARE SYSTEM
FOR FINANCIAL MANAGEMENT, PUNS
ON THE NAME BY SUBSTITUTING
STYLIZED PILLARS, YET THIS DOES
NOT EXPLAIN THE FIRM'S FUNCTION.
ART DIRECTOR: CLEMENT MOK
DESIGNER: SANDRA KOENIG
CLIENT: PILLAR CORPORATION

IN THIS 1986 LOGO FOR TRAVIS
CONSTRUCTION, A NAIL SUBSTITUTES
FOR THE INITIAL LETTER.
DESIGNER: WOODY PIRTLE,
PENTAGRAM
CLIENT: TRAVIS CONSTRUCTION

THE 1976 LOGO FOR MR. AND MRS.
AUBREY HAIR TAKES COMB TEETH AS
THE BASIS FOR THE LETTERFORMS.
DESIGNER: WOODY PIRTLE,
PENTAGRAM
CLIENT: MR. AND MRS. AUBREY HAIR

WITH AN ABSENCE OF TYPE, THE 1987
MEALS ON WHEELS LOGO IS A PURE
VISUAL PUN.
DESIGNER: MICHAEL OSTRO
CLIENT: ARCHDIOCESE OF HARTFORD

GARY

ABOVE: THE 1985 LOGO FOR GARY GRAY, COPYWRITER, BRILLIANTLY PLAYS OFF OF THE COMMON LETTERS IN HIS NAMES, USING THE COMMON PROOFREADER'S TRANSPOSITION MARK TO GIVE THE ENTIRE NAME—AND WITHOUT SETTING EXTRA TYPE.
DESIGNER: WOODY PIRTLE, PENTAGRAM
CLIENT: GARY GRAY

John Elliott Cellars Ltd, 11 Dover Street, Mayfair, London. Telephone : 01 493 5135 Wholesalers of Fine Wines & Champagne

Buvons, amis, et buvons à plein verre.
Enivrons-nous de ce nectar divin!
Après les Belles, sur la terre,
Rien n'est aimable que le vin;
Cette liqueur est de tout âge:
Buvons-en! Nargue du sage
Qui, le verre en main,
Le haussant soudain,
Craint, se ménage,
Et dit : holà!
Trop cela!
Holà!
La!
La!
La!
Car
Panard
A pour refrain:
Tout plein!
Plein!
Plein!
Plein!
Fêtons,
Célébrons
Sa mémoire;
Et, pour sa gloire,
Rions, chantons, aimons, buvons.

LEFT: THE 1977 SYMBOL, LABEL, AND POSTER FOR JOHN ELLIOT CELLARS FOLLOW THE TRADITION OF THE CALLIGRAMME—MORE THAN A MARK, IT IS A STATEMENT OF PRINCIPLES.
DESIGNERS: ALAN FLETCHER, PAUL ANTHONY
CLIENT: JOHN ELLIOT CELLARS

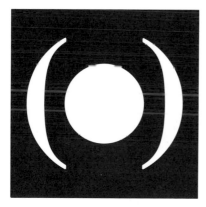

A PERIOD AND PARENTHESIS, USED FOR THIS 1986 LOGO FOR AN ASSOCIATION OF OPTICAL PRACTITIONERS, SERVES AS AN EYE AND EYEBALL.
DESIGNERS: MERVYN KURLANSKY, HERMAN LELIE, PENTAGRAM
CLIENT: SIGHT CARE

M PLUS M'S 1990 MARK FOR THE AIDS DEMONSTRATION, "A DAY WITHOUT ART," JOINS A STYLIZED FRAME WITH A UNIVERSAL SYMBOL FOR NOTHINGNESS.
DESIGNERS: TAKAAKI MATSUMOTO, MICHAEL MCGINN, M PLUS M INC.
CLIENT: VISUAL AIDS

ABOVE: THIS 1984 TYPOGRAPHIC
MAZE TESTS THE POWERS OF
PERCEPTION BUT OFFERS A VISUAL
GAME.
ART DIRECTOR/DESIGNER: CHRISTIAN
LaBARTHE, WAWA
CLIENT: SECRETARY OF STATE OF
CANADA, TRANSLATION BUREAU

ABOVE: THE 1987 MARK FOR
THE ONE SMART COOKIE
BAKERY COMBINES TWO VERY
FAMILIAR IMAGES INTO ONE
WITTY COMPOSITE.
ART DIRECTOR: RON SULLIVAN,
SULLIVAN/PERKINS
DESIGNERS: DIANA McKNIGHT,
MAX WRIGHT
ILLUSTRATOR: DIANA McKNIGHT
CLIENT: ONE SMART COOKIE

COCAINE

ABOVE: THIS STARK, NO-
FRILLS, 1987 NEWSPAPER
ADVERTISEMENT IS A PUN ON
THE IDEA THAT WHAT A
COCAINE USER SNORTS IS
MORE DANGEROUS THAN A
SIMPLE FINE, WHITE POWDER.
DESIGNER: TOM SCHWARTZ
AGENCY: DDB·NEEDHAM
WORLDWIDE INC.
CLIENT: PARTNERSHIP FOR A
DRUG-FREE AMERICA

MESA
GRILL

ABOVE: THE MESA GRILL IS A
RESTAURANT SERVING SOUTHWESTERN
FOOD IN NEW YORK CITY; A MESA IS A
FLAT PLAIN FOUND IN THE FAR WEST.
THE PUN ON THE WORD PLAYS OFF THE
LATTER IN THIS 1991 AD.
ART DIRECTOR: ALEXANDER ISLEY DESIGN
DESIGNER: ALEXANDER KNOWLTON
CLIENT: MESA GRILL

LEFT: SIMPLE, UNIVERSAL
SHAPES FOR THE HEART
CENTER CLINIC'S 1979 MARK,
THE VALENTINE'S HEART
AND THE BANDAGE ARE
UNMISTAKABLE.
DESIGNER: WOODY PIRTLE,
PENTAGRAM
CLIENT: HEART CENTER

DOUGLAS HARP TAKES A RATHER
LITERAL APPROACH TO A 1988 POSTER
ANNOUNCING DINNER AND MUSIC AT
THE CORNING GLASS CENTER.
DESIGNER/ILLUSTRATOR: DOUGLAS
HARP, CORNING CORPORATE DESIGN
CLIENT: CORNING GLASS CENTER
© 1988 CORNING INCORPORATED

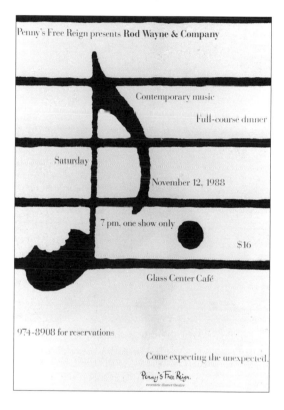

Penny's Free Reign presents **Rod Wayne & Company**

Contemporary music

Full-course dinner

Saturday

November 12, 1988

7 pm. one show only

$16

Glass Center Café

974-8908 for reservations

Come expecting the unexpected.

Penny's Free Reign.
eccentric dinner theatre

LIKE POLLEN, THE P DRIFTS OFF
INTO THE AIR IN THIS 1983 LOGO
FOR AN ALLERGY CLINIC.
DESIGNERS: STEVE GRIGG AND
DANIEL RUESCH, TANDEM STUDIOS
CLIENT: PROVO ALLERGY AND
ASTHMA CLINIC
©1983

PENTAGRAM'S 1985 DESIGN FOR
DAIMLER-BENZ'S ONE-HUNDREDTH
ANNIVERSARY OF THE MOTOR CAR
TRANSFORMS THE NUMBER INTO A CAR.
DESIGNER: ALAN FLETCHER, PENTAGRAM
CLIENT: DAIMLER-BENZ

THE 1988 MARK FOR
THE INSURANCE SCHOOL
INTEGRATES THE
LETTERFORM WITH A
MORTARBOARD CAP.
DESIGNER: MARK STEELE,
STEELE/PRESSON
CLIENT: THE INSURANCE
SCHOOL

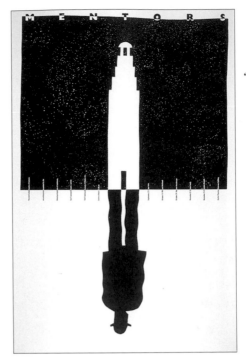

THIS 1989 POSTER, ANNOUNC-
ING AN ARCHITECTURAL
MENTORS LECTURE SERIES,
DRAWS UPON A VENERABLE
GRAPHIC TRICK KNOWN AS
"THE REVEALING SHADOW"
HERE THE SHADOW REVEALS
THE FORMAL AND CONCEPTUAL
RELATIONSHIP BETWEEN MAN
AND BUILDING.
DESIGNER: MICHAEL
VANDERBYL
CLIENT: SAN FRANCISCO
MUSEUM OF MODERN ART/SAN
FRANCISCO AIA

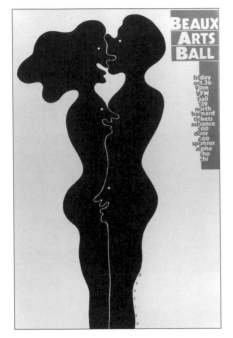

LANNY SOMMESE'S 1990 POSTER FOR
THE BEAUX ARTS BALL PUNS MALE
AND FEMALE ANATOMY. AT THE SAME
TIME, THE YIN/YANG AESTHETIC IS
REFLECTED IN THE TYPE TREATMENT
TO THE RIGHT.
DESIGNER: LANNY SOMMESE
CLIENT: BEAUX ARTS BALL,
UNIVERSITY OF PENNSYLVANIA

BELOW: THE 1984 MARK FOR
RICHMAN'S ZIPPER HOSPITAL
SEAMLESSLY COMBINES TWO
RECOGNIZABLE IMAGES.
ART DIRECTOR/DESIGNER:
STEVEN SNIDER
AGENCY: ROSSIN GREENBERG
SERONICK & HILL INC.
CLIENT: RICHMAN'S ZIPPER
HOSPITAL

THIS CAUTIONARY 1990 POSTER SERVES
AS A REMINDER THAT OZONE, THE MOST
PROTECTIVE LAYER OF THE EARTH'S
ATMOSPHERE, IS FAST DISSIPATING.
DESIGNER: DOUGLAS G. HARP,
HARP AND COMPANY
CLIENT: ADPSR

THE 1985 BILLBOARD FOR THE
FREDERICK RAUH & COMPANY INSUR-
ANCE BROKERAGE FIRM UNDERSCORES
THE ADVERTISING STATEMENT
THROUGH A GRAPHIC SUGGESTION OF
A DESTRUCTIVE FIRE.
ART DIRECTOR/DESIGNER: JIM JACOBS
CLIENT: FREDERICK RAUH & COMPANY

For those unforgettable evenings...

CHANNEL N°2

W G B H TV

Sexy pumps. Serious (but stylish) pumps. Power pumps. Fun flats. Street shoes. You want names? Bruno Magli. Salvatore Ferragamo. Anne Klein. Perry Ellis. Leather shoes. Snakeskin shoes (men love them). Suede shoes. For dancing. Dining. Job interviewing. Office politicing. Entrance making. More names. Ellen Tracy. Amalfi. We could go on. Liz Claiborne. Via Spiga. Bandolino. Brightly colored shoes. Like red. And purple. Citron (that's yellow to us). Of course, basic black. And brown. But have a little fun. Did we mention Allure. 9 West. Enzo. Come on. Come in. Try on twenty pairs. Oh, yes. Proxy. Esprit. So put your shoes on (if you like any of them). All our shoe departments are on sale. From Shoe-In on 1 to our Designer Shoe Salon on 4. Chicago. Like no other store in the world.

PUBLIC TELEVISION STATION WGBH IS
CHANNEL 2 IN BOSTON. USING THE 2
AS THE PRIMARY IDENTIFIER, CHRIS
PULLMAN FABRICATED IT IN VARIOUS
FORMS AS PROP AND TOY. WITHOUT
TRANSFORMING THE DIGIT INTO
SOMETHING OTHER THAN A NUMERAL,
PULLMAN USED IT TO SUGGEST A BIRD,
FOOTBALL, CHILDREN'S TOY, AND SO
ON IN THESE 1975–1979 ADS.
DESIGNERS: CHRIS PULLMAN,
GAYE KORBET
FABRICATOR: CONCEPT INDUSTRIES
CLIENT: WGBH BOSTON

LEFT: FOR THE 1990 JACKET OF ALL
YOU WHO SLEEP TONIGHT, A BOOK OF
POEMS, CHIP KIDD USED ANTON
STANKOWSKI'S 1930 PHOTOGRAPH
TO SUGGEST A MAN AND WOMAN
TOGETHER IN BED.
ART DIRECTOR: CAROL CARSON
DESIGNER: CHIP KIDD
PHOTOGRAPHER: ANTON STANKOWSKI
CLIENT: ALFRED A. KNOPF INC.

ECLIPSE

THE 1985 LOGO FOR ECLIPSE
REFLECTIVE GLASS LITERALLY
TRANSLATES THE ECLIPSE CONCEPT.
DESIGNER: JEFF KIMBLE
ILLUSTRATOR: SUE POTVIN
AGENCY: ZAPIECKI & PARTNERS INC.
CLIENT: LIBBEY-OWENS-FORD CO.

IN THIS 1984 PARODY OF POST-
MODERN ARCHITECTURE, MICHAEL
VANDERBYL IS ALSO MAKING A
PUN USING ARCHITECTURAL FORMS
TO ANTHROPOMORPHIZE AN
INANIMATE STRUCTURE.
DESIGNER: MICHAEL VANDERBYL
CLIENT: SELF

BELOW: MCRAY MAGLEBY'S 1989 AIDS
POSTER USES THE CRUCIFIX TO SUGGEST
GENITALIA AND TO PROTEST REPRESSION OF
THE FACTS ON THIS KILLER DISEASE.
DESIGNER: MCRAY MAGLEBY, BYU GRAPHICS
CLIENT: SHOSHIN SOCIETY

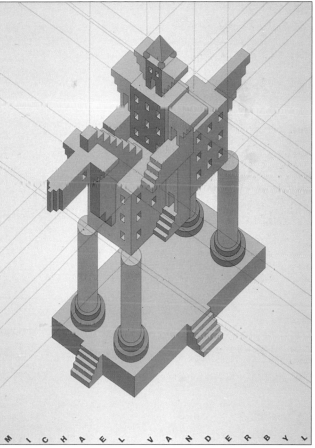

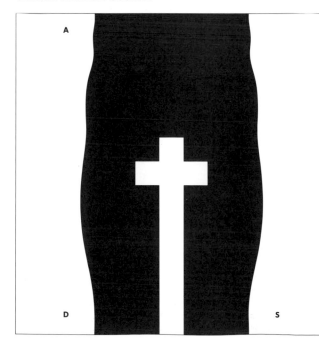

RIGHT: THIS 1976 PIECE IS
A LITERAL PLAY ON THE
TITLE CONCERTO RETITLED.
ART DIRECTOR/DESIGNER:
LYNN DREESE BRESLIN,
BOB DEFRIN
PHOTOGRAPHER: CHRIS
CALLIS
CLIENT: ATLANTIC
RECORDS

ZOLO® TOY, 1989
DESIGNERS: SANDRA HIGASHI
& BYRON GLASER
CLIENT: ZOLO, INC.
© HIGASHI GLASER DESIGN

CUBIZM GAME, 1991
DESIGNERS: SANDRA HIGASHI
& BYRON GLASER
CLIENT: ZOLO, INC.

PUZZLE HEAD PUZZLE, 1991
DESIGNER: RICHARD MCGUIRE
CLIENT: RICHARD MCGUIRE

TOYS AND PLAYTHINGS

A few years back, a prestigious New York art gallery mounted a Christmas show of artists' toys. In fact, the number of what one might call serious "Sunday toy makers" was impressive, but not really surprising, for artists are inveterate toy makers. For example, few visitors to New York's Whitney Museum of American Art have failed to notice and be smitten by Alexander Calder's circus. His delightful animals, clowns, and circus accoutrements fashioned from pieces of twisted wire and old fabric are a treat for young and old (indeed, perhaps more for the latter, who can thoroughly relate to the artist's unpretentiousness). Calder made his toys as an extention of his creative being. Other artists in the New York

gallery show made toys and playthings not for resale but either as respites from their daily routines or as extensions of their canvases or sculptures. In fact, many of these objects are reminders that before the advent of GI Joe, Barbie, and Mutant Ninja Turtles, toys were unpretentious, functional artworks intended to be used, abused, and enjoyed.

Graphic designers and illustrators are no less able, ready, or willing to make toys for limited, personal use. But since commercial graphic artists tend to have a little more business savvy than their fine-arts counterparts, it should come as no surprise that some of these inventions make it into the public arena. Indeed, as the counterpoint to mass-produced toys, and consistent with the boutique mentality of today's retail marketers, certain entrepreneurs are successfully marketing "artist's" toys to the public. Among the most popular is B. Glaser and S. Higarashi's Zolo. Spiritually influenced by the Italian Memphis Group's preference for wild colors and cartoon shapes, Zolo is a collection of amorphic shapes and objects, which, when pieced together (like a sophisticated Mr. Potato Head), become uniquely funny figures. Unlike traditionally packaged toys, Zolo comes in boxes that echo the humor of the game inside rather than pandering to the worst instincts of the buyer and seller. Drawing further on their skill as graphic designers, Glaser and Higarashi have also issued Cubizm, a block game that employs wittily cropped and fragmented graphic elements in a delightfully random composition. Likewise, illustrator Richard McGuire has applied his fascination for comic doodles to his Puzzle Head game, a set of interlocking faces that come together as a single composition. In each case, the marketing is secondary to the joy of toy making.

Similarly, some designers use toy-making techniques and special effects to imbue their commercial designs with playful allure, almost like puns of toys. Cheri Dorr's CD package for MTV combines Post-Modern typeplay with

CATCHER IN THE RYE BATHROOM TISSUE
ART DIRECTOR/DESIGNER: TOM
KLUEPFUL, DRENTTEL/DOYLE PARTNERS
CLIENT: ID MAGAZINE

MASKS GIVEN TO PARTICIPANTS IN A
HALLOWEEN SALES CONFERENCE, 1986
ART DIRECTOR: CLEMENT MOK
DESIGNER: JILL SAVINI
ILLUSTRATOR: STEVEN GUARNACCIA
CLIENT: APPLE COMPUTER INC.

three-dimensional tactility. Steven Guarnaccia's die-cut invitation to an exhibition of his work is basically a mini-mask that unfolds to create a three-dimensional sculpture. Guarnaccia (see interview, page 152) bases much of his graphic design and illustration on the influence of old toys, which he collects almost obsessively. Indeed, the masks shown here, which Guarnaccia designed for Clement Mok at Apple Computers, are derived exclusively from this source.

TOY AS PUN   The popularity of the Sharper Image store chain in recent years is in direct response to the needs of baby-boomers (the most affluent generation in memory), who grew up with an excess of toys and have the taste for more. This, combined with an increase in electronic gadgetry, has created a new market. These grown-up toy stores are a kind of hybrid of art or museum shops and novelty boutiques, influenced in recent years by a rise in "artists" products and wares in the marketplace. By now, everyone who's anyone owns a Michael Graves teapot, which is really a caricature of a teapot, or a Philippe Starck juicer, which though it looks like a scrunched silver king crab is actually quite functional. Jumping on the bandwagon, certain graphic designers have diversified into the gadget or *tchotchke* market with great zeal and vibrato.

In terms of toylike products, one might have thought T-shirts would become a designer's niche, or that novelties like Stephen Doyle's *Catcher in the Rye* facial tissues might be a close second. Actually, watches are the most common product to emerge from the offices of contemporary graphic designers. Indeed, with the advent

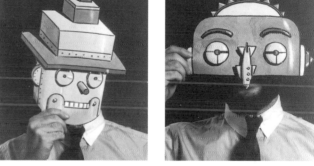

of the inexpensive designer Swatch Watch, watches have replaced jeans as the preeminent haute design manifestation of the Post-Modern era. And since a watch is a watch, designers have sought to give meaning to their concoctions by making them into puns. M&Co., Drenttel Doyle Partners, Doublespace, and Spot Design have also fortuitously timed their entries into the market in perfect synch with the decline in popularity of the digital watch.

As book outlets decrease and the book market becomes more competitive, publishers are testing new gimmicks. Random House, for example, announced that it will release a line of scented books. The obvious ones on gardening

MINIATURE GOLF BOOK COVER, 1987
ART DIRECTOR: JIM WAGMAN
DESIGNER: HELENE SILVERMAN
CLIENT: ABBEVILLE PRESS

BOWL O RAMA BOOK COVER, 1986
DESIGNER/PHOTOGRAPHER:
H. THOMAS STEELE
CLIENT: ABBEVILLE PRESS

PRINT CRAFT TRUCK, 1990
DESIGNERS: CHARLES SPENCER
ANDERSON, DAN OLSON
CLIENT: PRINT CRAFT

"TEN ONE FOUR" WATCH, 1987
DESIGNERS: TIBOR KALMAN,
MAIRA KALMAN
CLIENT: M&CO.

and cooking may be cloying but at least make sense; but what about sports books? Ugh. Meanwhile, for a few years Abbeville Press has published its "nine by nine" series of books on emphemera and popular Americana, which usually include covers as toys. Two of them are tactile puns: *Bowl O Rama: The Visual Arts of Bowling*, designed by Tommy Steele, has two die-cut holes in the bowling ball appearing on the cover, and the title for *Miniature Golf*, designed by Helene Silverman, is printed on acetate over a patch of "real" Astroturf.

One final note on toys: The most satisfying play for a designer is a toy used in real life. For Charles Spencer Anderson, seeing his design for Print Craft enlarged on the side of a truck is like driving the real version of that Tonka Truck he played with as a kid.

"LIFE SIZE" WATCH, 1990
DESIGNER: DREW HODGES,
SPOT DESIGN
ILLUSTRATOR: GENE GRIEF
CLIENT: ARTWORX WATCHES,
ROLAND MARKETING

"FUEL GAUGE," WATCH, 1990
CREATIVE DIRECTOR/
ART DIRECTOR/DESIGNER:
TOM KLUEPFEL
CLIENT: DRENTTEL DOYLE
PARTNERS

"LULU" WATCH, 1987
DESIGNERS: TIBOR KALMAN,
ALEXANDER ISLEY
CLIENT: M&CO.

"HAND AND SHOE" WATCH,
1989
DESIGNER: DREW HODGES,
SPOT DESIGN
ILLUSTRATOR: GENE GRIEF
CLIENT: ARTWORX WATCHES,
ROLAND MARKETING

"SHUTTER SPEED" WATCH,
1990
CREATIVE DIRECTOR/
ART DIRECTOR/ DESIGNER:
TOM KLUEPFEL
CLIENT: DRENTTEL/ DOYLE
PARTNERS

"CHICKEN & RICE" WATCH,
1990
CREATIVE DIRECTOR:
MONICA HALPERT
ART DIRECTORS: JANE
KOSSTRIN AND DAVID
STERLING, DOUBLESPACE
DESIGNERS: JANE KOSSTRIN
AND JAMIE OLIVERI
CLIENT: BIG TIME LICENSING
AND MTV NETWORKS

4 Deja Vu All Over Again

FOR MOVIE SHOWTIMES & LOCATIONS FAST
CALL
777-FILM
213 714
"OUR PHONES ARE NEVER BUSY!"
A NEW FREE SERVICE! KLOS 95.5

BOTTOM: FLASH CARDS, SUCH AS THIS 1990 EXAMPLE FOR 777-FILM, WERE USED LONG BEFORE MORE MODERN TECHNOLOGY ALLOWED FOR MORE SOPHISTICATED APPROACHES.
DESIGNER: DREW HODGES, SPOT DESIGN
CLIENT: PROMOFONE

NOSTALGIC WIT Nostalgia. It sounds like an ailment—neuritis, neuralgia, nostalgia. Take a bromo and call me in the morning. In fact, the word was coined in the seventeenth century to describe a severe illness brought about by homesickness afflicting soldiers during the Thirty Years War. In addition to fits of melancholia induced by battle, protracted absences from hearth and home caused these young warriors to experience intense stomach pains and nausea—no laughing matter, to be sure. Yet by the nineteenth century, other terms replaced nostalgia in the medical sense, and the term came to signify a romantic memory of, or dreamlike return to, a more sublime and innocent time and place in history.

We have all been nostalgic for something lost, misplaced, or simply experienced and fondly remembered. But nostalgia is not exclusively a recollection of one's *own* past, but rather of any number of depersonalized and idealized pasts having occurred as far back as eons ago and as recently as yesterday. In art, for example, the late-nineteenth-century pre-Raphaelite Brotherhood of painters, illustrators, and designers who influenced an aspect of turn-of-the-century English decorative art, returned to what they saw as a venerable aesthetic predating the perceived artistic malaise of their own time. They adopted styles and themes that conjured up Merrie Olde England, complete with its Knights of the Round Table, in an attempt to rekindle values long gone but still appreciated. Their vision was intended as a gateway toward new discovery, but rarely resulted in much more than a stylistic conceit—which, incidentally, became a rather comic conceit that might be referred to as the Prince Valiant approach to art. Indeed, reprising the past for inspiration can be a problem if applied without critical perspective, for the past is not the present, and never will be. Used for its own sake, nostalgia quickly becomes a creative and emotional crutch.

Nonetheless, nostalgia will continue to be popular as long as people choose to experience the past voyeuristically. For this reason, it's also a big business today. Writing about nostalgia as a marketing strategy, Randall Rothenberg reported in the *New York Times* that "the way it

was is the way it is." Marketers acutely under-stand that trading on a legacy, even a fictional or manufactured one, gives consumers of certain products the confidence needed to make their buying choices. The past serves as a pedigree for a company or product, and design is the princi-pal means of communicating this past. However, there was a time when a longing for the *future*— and a rejection of the past—held the same mass appeal as nostalgia does today. The 1939 New York World's Fair was billed "The World of Tomorrow," and predicted the wonders of

American civilization twenty years hence. To-morrowland was once Disneyland's most excit-ing attraction, offering speculation on commuter space travel and other semifulfilled technological advancements. Throughout America, atomic power was the symbol of progress, and "progress," said General Electric, was their "most important product." In design, everything from logos to exhibitions exalted the *atomania*. This craze for the future was also fueled by the success of manned space travel, which reached its zenith with an American landing on the moon

SINCE 1988, JERRY JOHNSON HAS
USED THE SIDES OF OLD BROOKLYN
BUILDINGS TO MAKE MAMMOTH
HAND-PAINTED SIGNS THAT MIMIC
THE WALLSIDE ADS OF THE 1940S
AND 1950S AND SATIRIZE THE
SUBSEQUENT CHANGES IN AMERICAN
POP AND MATERIAL CULTURE.
DESIGNER: JERRY JOHNSON
CLIENT: ORANGE OUTDOOR
ADVERTISING

IN THIS 1988 COLLAGE FOR HBE BANK
FACILITIES, CLAES OLDENBURG–
INSPIRED SCALE CHANGES COMBINE
WITH SILLY NOSTALGIC STOCK
CHARACTERS TO ILLUSTRATE THE IDEA
THAT WHILE A BANK IS NOT TIED TO
TRENDS OR FASHIONS, THIS UNIQUE
SERVICE WILL UPDATE A BANK'S
BUSINESS PROCEDURES WITHOUT
DISTURBING THE STATUS QUO.
ART DIRECTOR: RON LOPEZ
DESIGNER: DAVID BARTELS, BARTELS
& CARSTENS INC.

Why should your bank go anywhere? It's doing very well just where it is. In fact, if you had to pick a new location, the one you're in is the one you'd pick.

There are problems, however. As great as your location is, the building your bank is in isn't. It needs more than a facelift. It needs a complete uplift.

And that's why we're running this ad. To tell you that the only move you have to make is to pick up the telephone and call HBE.

With our Smart Design℠ concept we can uplift and update your bank without upsetting your business. By combining

WHY HBE IS PERFECT FOR BANKS THAT AREN'T GOING ANYWHERE.

the disciplines of planning, architecture, engineering and construction in a synergistic way, the Smart Design approach provides you with modernization and improved efficiency in your present location.

How can you be sure that HBE's Smart Design℠ process is the way for you? Simple. Just call Mike Dolan, Senior Vice President, at 1-800-234-9393. You'll find how far you can go without making a move.

HBE
Bank Facilities
A Division of HBE Corporation.
11330 Olive Street Rd • St. Louis, MO 63141

THIS 1982 REVIVAL OF THE OLD BANK
CALENDAR (GIVEN AWAY FOR FREE IN
THE YEARS BEFORE THE HIGH COST OF
PAPER AND WASTE-CONSCIOUSNESS)
IS HERE STAPLED TO A DIE-CUT
ILLUSTRATION OF A STEREOTYPICAL
1950S KITCHEN.
DESIGNER: KENNETH KNEITEL
MANUFACTURER: EASY ACES

TOP LEFT: BY MAKING AN ICON OF A SILLY, ANONYMOUS FACE, THIS CAMPAIGN TO PROMOTE ADRIAN, "THE GURU OF NEW WAVE CONSCIOUSNESS," MAKES THE MUNDANE MONUMENTAL.
DESIGNER: DAVID ART WALES
CLIENT: SELF

BOTTOM LEFT: REACTOR'S 1989 "FUN WITH COMPUTERS" POSTER PROVES THAT ENVISIONING THE PRESENT IS NOT AS MUCH FUN AS USING THE PAST AS A COUNTERPOINT.
DESIGNER: LOUIS FISHAUF
AGENCY: REACTOR
CLIENT: TOPIX

CHARLES SPENCER ANDERSON REVIVES OLD COMMERCIAL ART AND USES IT AS THE BASIS OF A PERSONAL STYLE, WHICH IS SOMETIMES APPROPRIATE, AS IN THE 1990 No-Sex Handbook, AND AT OTHER TIMES MORE THAN JUST A STYLISH CONCEIT.
DESIGNERS: CHARLES SPENCER ANDERSON, DAN OLSON
CLIENT: WARNER BOOKS

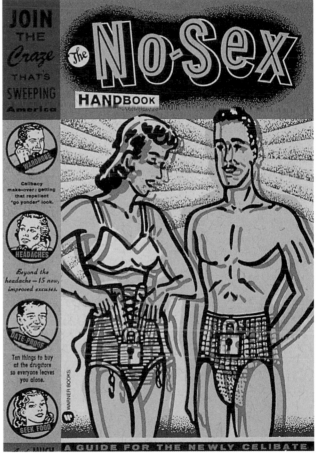

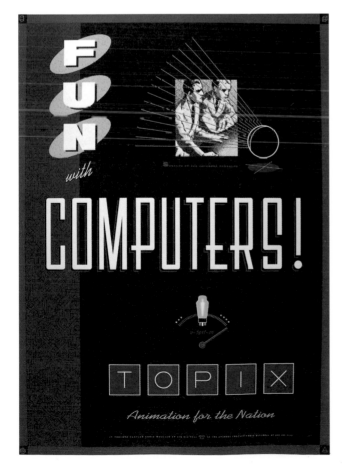

LEFT: SCOTT MEDNICK'S 1989 POSTER BORROWS FROM BOWLING'S ONGOING GRAPHIC STYLE.
CREATIVE DIRECTOR/ART DIRECTOR: SCOTT A. MEDNICK
DESIGNER: DANIEL J. SIMON
ILLUSTRATORS: DANIEL J. SIMON, CATHY LINSTROM
COPYWRITERS: PETER THORNBURGH, DANIEL J. SIMON
CLIENT: ART DIRECTORS CLUB OF LOS ANGELES

ART BRAND BUTTONS IS HYBRID
RETRO: A 1980 MIX OF 1930S SIGN
PAINTING, 1950S BUTTONS, AND
REMBRANDT ADDS UP TO NOSTALGIA
THAT COVERS ALL BASES.
DESIGNER/ILLUSTRATOR:
KENNETH KNEITEL
MANUFACTURER: EASY ACES

CHARLES SPENCER ANDERSON'S 1990
OLD ADVERTISING CUTS FROM A–Z
RETURNS HIS OTHERWISE PRIVATE-
DOMAIN ADVERTISING ART BACK INTO
THE PUBLIC DOMAIN—AT $19.95
("COMPLETE," OF COURSE).
ART DIRECTOR/DESIGNER: CHARLES
SPENCER ANDERSON
CLIENT: FRENCH PAPER COMPANY
COPYWRITER: DONN CARSTENS
CLIENT: HBE BANK FACILITIES

LEFT: TOM BONAURO KNOWS THAT
LASSIE (OR A LASSIE LOOK-ALIKE) HAS
UNTOLD POWERS, WHICH MAY ACCOUNT
FOR WHY THIS CANINE IS USED TO
ADVERTISE A 1989 ART EXHIBITION.
ART DIRECTOR/DESIGNER: TOM BONAURO
CLIENT: TODD OLDHAM

in 1969. Space, "the final frontier," not only gave us *Star Trek* and *The Jetsons*, but also Stanley Kubrick's epic *2001: A Space Odyssey*, which influenced futuristic styles in everything from graphics to clothing to cars. But *2001* was also the beginning of our collective backslide into a nostalgic obsession. Evoking millennial fears, like those experienced at the turn of the nineteenth century, when it was prophesized that industrialization would lead to the end of civilization, *2001* suggested that the future wasn't (or wouldn't be) all it had been cracked up to be: Things could indeed go wrong. Warnings of environmental hazards were routinely ignored and written off as the ravings of crackpots despite the physical evidence that progress was taking its ecological toll. Even a 1964 issue of *Mad* magazine, in one of its more prescient comic features, satirically cautioned about the industrial world's growing waste-disposal problems, suggesting that space shuttles would soon transport refuse into space and leave rings of garbage around the earth and other planets. By the 1970s, fascination with the future began to turn to skepticism. And, finally, with the end of the Vietnam War in 1974, attention turned fully to a new enemy: the byproducts of progress.

Without the prospect of a glorious future to hold the imagination, an idealized past was revived to anchor mass hopes and dreams to something tried and true, with mass media as the conduit and graphic design a principal tool. The first era to be so revived was, ironically, the 1950s, a decade during which Senator Joseph McCarthy had run roughshod over American freedom, rock and roll had been outlawed in

schools as aboriginal and animalistic, and African Americans had suffered under Jim Crow in the American South. But the myth portrayed on television series like *Laverne and Shirley* and *Happy Days*, in movies like *American Graffiti*, and, yes, even in the advertising and graphic design of the period, instead highlighted the fictional heroes of mass media, as well as such pop-cultural ephemera as hoola hoops, Davy Crockett hats,

MICHAEL MABRY'S 1990 PROMOTION
BOOKLET FOR STRATHMORE PAPER,
<u>AMERICAN ICONS</u>, DRAWS UPON THE
GRAPHIC IMAGES OF SOME OF
AMERICA'S MOST SUCCESSFUL
COMPANIES.
ART DIRECTOR: MICHAEL MABRY
DESIGNERS: MICHAEL MABRY,
MARGIE CHU
ILLUSTRATOR: MELISSA GRIMES
AGENCY: KEILER ADVERTISING
CLIENT: STRATHMORE PAPER
COMPANY

EVOKING THE PAST IN AN OTHERWISE
CONTEMPORARY DESIGN IS OFTEN A
MEANS OF CONVEYING A MESSAGE
SIMPLY AND ECONOMICALLY. THE
1985 COVER ILLUSTRATION FOR
<u>SQUARE MEALS</u>, A BOOK ABOUT REAL
HOME COOKING, SUGGESTS THE ERA OF
THE HOUSEBOUND HOMEMAKER.
ART DIRECTOR: SARA EISENMAN
DESIGNER: KAREN KATZ
CLIENT: ALFRED A. KNOPF

jukeboxes, and '57 Chevys. These and other period symbols were combined into a stylized "retro" graphic vocabulary that was not only unthreatening but also rather silly, especially in light of other, more imaginative contemporary graphic styles.

Many critics have branded the 1950s as an uptight decade, noting its lack of humor. But the nostalgia of the late 1970s and 1980s has had a rehabilitating effect, allowing a generation who never experienced the 1950s to look at the period

from a different, more rose-colored vantage point than was available to those who grew up in it. Many 1950s graphic images and letterforms, especially the emblematic scripts, novelty typefaces, trade characters (like Speedy Alka-Seltzer and Reddy Kilowatt) and decorative design ornaments (including liver-shaped lozenges) were reapplied in entirely new contexts. Some design-

ers used these images as codes, serving, for example, as satiric devices counterpointing contemporary fashions. Some designers used the graphic forms for their inherent humor, and still others for the pure aesthetic pleasure of working with appealing graphic forms that would otherwise be considered out of bounds.

Although there is currently a trend toward revived 1960s psychedelia, most subsequent nostalgic direction has been backwards. Graphic ornaments from the 1940s, 1930s, and even the 1920s have become once again ripe for the picking. Indeed, each of these periods had a more or less identifiable graphic style or code, though one often spilled over into the other (which is understandable—there is no reason to expect graphic trends to respect such calendar-driven notions as decades). During the 1920s, the remnants of Art Nouveau gave way to Art Moderne

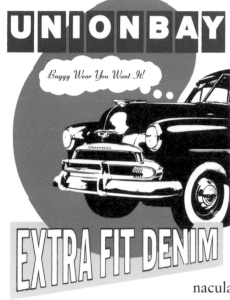

(or Art Deco) and, more lastingly, the progressively Modern. During the 1930s, Cubistic Art Deco was ubiquitous in Europe, while a variant known as Streamlining developed in the United States. Owing to World War II, the early 1940s were visually austere, yet the late 1940s saw the convergence of many previous stylistic manifestations. Tom Wolfe aptly describes the present confluence of design styles as having derived from a "big closet," which designers turned into a rummage sale, with outmoded style manuals available for pennies and a priceless supply of old forms on hand as well.

It is worth noting that this is not a new phenomenon. The psychedelic poster artists of the late 1960s referred to themselves as "pack rats," borrowing (or in today's art parlance, *appropriating*) past imagery because it either had aesthetic or psychological value or was just simply funny. The new designer pack rats' motives are similar, although their chosen language is quite different from that of their predecessors.

Despite psychedelia's appropriation of East Indian, Native American, Vienna Secessionist, and American Victorian design elements, its graphic language, which also included a rainbow color palette and curvilinear, drug-induced shapes, turned into a

distinctly original design language. Indeed, over time, and after intense mainstream co-opting, it became the ambient voice for a youthful, sex, drugs, and rock 'n' roll–inspired constituency. More precisely, psychedelia borrowed from the vernaculars of previous times and places to become the vernacular of its own time and place. We

might note here that vernacular is common, everyday language, which is actually how one might define commercial art or graphic design, since their purpose is to communicate to a mass audience in a language that will be understandable to all.

VERNACULAR HUMOR

In the 1980s, the word *vernacular* was used rather imprecisely by graphic designers to distinguish naive, poorly designed, or undesigned printed manifestations from *premeditated* graphic design, or what are now haughtily referred to as graphic communications. This is, of course, a subjective hierarchical notion based on comparative levels of taste, training, skill, and talent. In fact, work done without an aesthetic sense or design plan, such as a paper coffee cup or a luncheonette menu showing some stock scene of the Parthenon and typeset in some ugly, "default" typeface is not graphic design per se, but common, commercial job printing. Conversely, a paper coffee cup and menu featuring, for example, the OH LA LA logo *is* graphic design, because a graphic design-

er (not a printer or sign painter) produced it. Vernacular is considered inherently funny not just because most old fashions are considered funny years after the fact but because they represent a time before designers were sophisticated professionals. The vernacular is therefore easy to satirize, because in an era of design sophistication, it is so charmingly naive.

In the 1960s, American Pop artists began appropriating commercial art, making it monumental and thereby giving it the status of high art. Soup cans, billboards, gas station identity systems, and so on were heralded by art's avant-garde as the "true" American vernacular. Likewise, taking a cue from Robert Venturi's landmark analysis of indigenous commercial architecture (i.e., kitsch), *Learning from Las Vegas*, graphic designers during the 1980s focused on the newly discovered vernacular, either as the brunt of their humor (by exaggerating and distorting these forms) or as a wellspring for new and old processes. In both cases, the unpretentious vernacular was elevated to an *au courant* style, a witty style, because the forms being quoted were so dated that they cannot be straight-facedly used without some infusion of irony. Moreover, it was a unique style, because most trained designers would be hesitant to step

LIKE A REBUS, M&CO. IN 1986
APPROPRIATED UNAMBIGUOUS STOCK
CUTS FROM THE YELLOW PAGES.
DESIGNERS: ALEXANDER ISLEY,
TIBOR KALMAN, M&CO.
CLIENT: RESTAURANT FLORENT

USING EXISTING STOCK PHOTOGRAPHY
AS BACKGROUND, M&CO.'S 1986
"FIRM IDENTITY" HAS A
DEVIL-MAY-CARE ATTITUDE.
DESIGNERS: STEPHEN DOYLE,
TIBOR KALMAN, M&CO.
CLIENT: M&CO.

BELOW: THE DESIGN OF PLAYING
CARDS HAS A LONG HISTORY,
DATING BACK TO MEDIEVAL TIMES.
IN THIS 1989 BOOK JACKET, THE
STYLE OF THE MOST
CONVENTIONAL CARD IS
TRANSFORMED INTO A STRIKING
JACKET IMAGE.
ART DIRECTOR: JACKIE SEOW
DESIGNER: JON VALK
CLIENT: FIRESIDE BOOKS, SIMON
& SCHUSTER

Dear Ronnie
The White House.

NOTHING IS MORE VERNACULAR THAN
CHILDREN'S HANDWRITING. IN 1985,
ART CHANTRY USED HIS NINE-YEAR-
OLD NEPHEW'S SCRAWL FOR THE
COVER OF A RECORD BY SHELLY AND
THE CRUSTACEANS.
DESIGNER: ART CHANTRY
CLIENT: THE CRUSTACEANS

THIS VINTAGE 1897 PHOTO IS THE
PERFECT METAPHOR FOR THIS 1987
ANNOUNCEMENT FOR A COMPETITION
DEVOTED TO PROJECTS THAT BRIDGE
PERSONAL AND PROFESSIONAL LIVES.
DESIGNER: MICHAEL BEIRUT
CLIENT: ARCHITECTURAL LEAGUE OF
NEW YORK

EVER WONDER WHO DESIGNED THE
COMMON OPEN AND CLOSED SIGNS?
WAS IT SOME STRUGGLING ARTIST
WHO WENT ON TO GREATER GLORY? IN
THIS 1988 VACATION ANNOUNCEMENT,
THE DESIGNER USES THE EMBLEMATIC
FORMS TO COMMUNICATE A SOMEWHAT
MORE COMPLEX MESSAGE.
DESIGNERS: JILLY SIMONS, JOE
VANDERBOS
CLIENT: CONCRETE

into the muck of old-fashioned commercial art without imbuing it with a sense of the absurd.

Nostalgic art can be vernacular, but not all vernacular is nostalgic art. In the 1960s, Pop artists were not recalling the past but rehabilitating then-current packaging and signage. Similarly, when New York's M&Co. designs a restaurant menu to look like it was slapped together at a print shop instead of being designed at all, it is intended not as a nostalgic evocation of the vernacular but rather as a subtle critique of the opulence and waste inherent in much contemporary graphic design. In fact, M&Co.'s menus for two New York restaurants, Bellevues and Restaurant Florent, serve two purposes, giving the restaurants warm and witty personalities to contrast starkly with their excessively chic competition, and showing by example that not all graphic design needs costly production tricks to be effective. Therefore, M&Co.'s appropriation of the vernacular at once codifies a new kind of chic and a certain kind of environmental responsibility. Employing the vernacular has also provided M&Co. with a starting point for a distinctive design methodology, involving a breakdown of the popular aesthetics canon with the aim of changing the way clients and customers perceive and respond to printed communications.

Charles Spencer Anderson, on the other hand, emerged as a leading proponent of nostalgic humor during the late 1980s while with the Duffy Design Group of Minneapolis. Armed with a few rare 1930s matchbook advertising manuals, Anderson gave new life to old comic stock vignettes, or what Paul Rand terms "the absolute worst of commercial art. The stuff we

SERIES OF "HOWELL CUTS,"
USED TO ENLIVEN
COMMERCIAL JOB PRINTING,
1929.

[the Modernists] fought so hard to eliminate." Rand has been practicing for half a century and has lived through many stylistic periods while steadfastly maintaining a distinctive graphic personality based on an aesthetic and intellectual philosophy that transcends fashion. For him, these comic cuts are not vernacular gems but purile clichés without wit or aesthetic value. He sees no inherent joke in them, nor any justifiable purpose for their being revived except as a refuge for those without original ideas. But Anderson was in his early 20s when he became a practicing graphic designer, and so had limited knowledge of design history, which in turn meant he didn't realize (or at least had no idea *why*) these outmoded forms were considered anathema by the veteran Modernists. But his funny bone was quite honestly tickled by them—for Anderson, the cuts represent an appealing aspect of popular culture, inherently funny and curiously alluring, especially in contrast to graphic design that takes itself too seriously.

For decades, Dover Books has been publishing a variety of stock-cut compendia, from pre-Victorian engravings to 1930s Art Deco vignettes. Some of the same cuts that Anderson exploits have been reproduced previously in Dover's copyright-free volumes, and many designers from various schools of thought have drawn either inspiration or full unaltered images from these books, thus adding an element of humor to otherwise dry solutions. These period stock cuts can function like seasoning, spicing up a spare or low-budget design, yet, like all seasonings, they should not be applied in excess—for when overused, one is left with a headache.

THE CURSE OF THE CLICHÉ Technically, a cliché is a pattern in clay, which is why clay-based stereotyped printing plates are referred to in the argot of printing as clichés. Of course, a cliché also refers to a saying, idea, or image that is used over and over until it becomes trite. In Europe, however, the term is used to describe the small, ready-made illustrations sold by printers and typesetters. For our purposes, a visual cliché is something seen so often, and therefore so immediately understandable, that it does not require translation or interpretation. The problem with a cliché, however, is that something so familiar is easy to ignore. Moreover, using clichés usually results in predictable solutions. Yet when compared to verbal platitudes, *visual* clichés are slightly more effective, because familiar visual cues aid in quick comprehension.

When used as an element of an original idea, a cliché can be a mnemonic device that enhances meaning. Take, for instance, some very common and universal symbols, like a skull and crossbones, Uncle Sam, and a cornucopia. By themselves, they are recognizable but not inherently interesting or witty. But when placed in absurd or incongruous contexts, these clichés become keys for unlocking less accessible messages. Clichés are thus used best when they transcend their own limited meanings.

Clichés can be transformed into dynamic symbols by scale changes, odd juxtapositions, and radical distortions: A skull and crossbones becomes funnier when a knife and fork replace the bones; Uncle Sam appears less conventional when his stovepipe hat turns into lettering; and a cornucopia—well, actually it's quite difficult to transform a cornucopia into anything *but* a cliché! In addition, clichés can be made fresh simply by the physical nature of a design and its context. And even the old cornucopia can appear somewhat original given the right application of color or type.

The surrealist painter Max Ernst used trite nineteenth-century magazine engravings as the

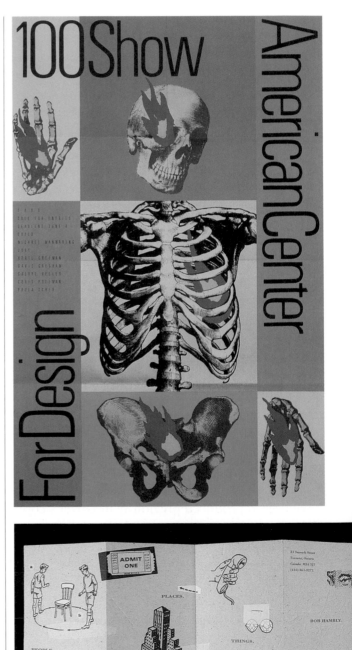

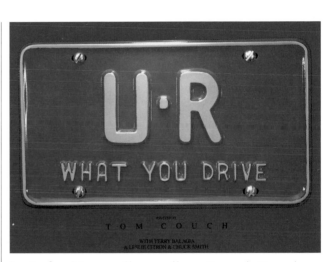

basis for his wordless collage "novels," such as his masterpiece of absurdity, *La Semaine De Bonte.* By cutting and seamlessly pasting animal heads, flowers, and body parts onto other disparate images, he made new visual discoveries. Doing so, he transformed a collection of visual clichés into exciting representations with new meanings. Historically speaking, collage is one of the primary media through which many other artists have transformed visual clichés into uniquely imaginative, often humorous conceptions. Indeed, German Dadaists Raul Hausmann, Hannah Hoch, and George Grosz all borrowed their graphic props from a wide variety of commercial printer's manuals, which were then constructed into seemingly random compositions that were really sophisticated, premeditated political and social commentaries. John Heartfield, another leading Dadaist, combined original photographs and stock (or clichéd) photographs into montages, resulting in some of the most acerbic and memorable political propaganda of the 1930s.

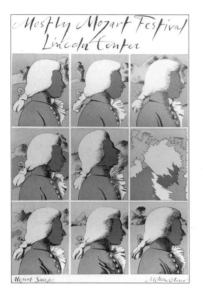

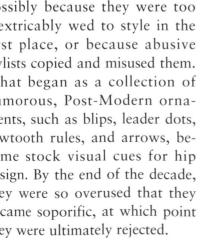

Someone once wrote that the truths of today are the clichés of tomorrow. Indeed, given the spate of design annuals on the market, many truly original ideas quickly devolve into clichés because of designers' habits of following stylistic and conceptual trends. During the 1980s, some very unique design conceits became clichés, possibly because they were too inextricably wed to style in the first place, or because abusive stylists copied and misused them. What began as a collection of humorous, Post-Modern ornaments, such as blips, leader dots, sawtooth rules, and arrows, became stock visual cues for hip design. By the end of the decade, they were so overused that they became soporific, at which point they were ultimately rejected.

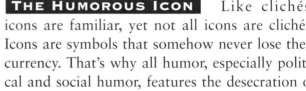

THE HUMOROUS ICON

Like clichés, icons are familiar, yet not all icons are clichés. Icons are symbols that somehow never lose their currency. That's why all humor, especially political and social humor, features the desecration of icons as a recurring device. Few things are more outrageous than a caustic comedian's impersonation of a famous (or infamous) politician or world leader. Indeed, when caricaturists unmask a public figure through visual exaggeration they've exposed folly more efficiently than virtually any investigative news story about malfeasance.

The Old Testament tacitly gives its approval to this kind of caricature when Moses urges the obliteration of false icons. Yet icon desecration in Christianity is

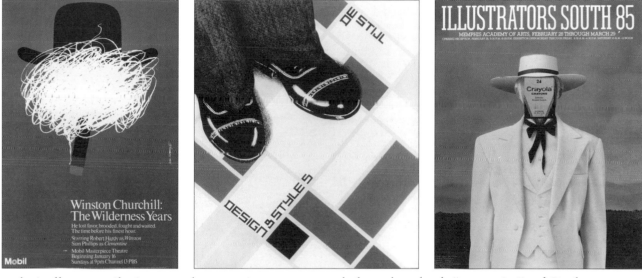

technically a sacrilegious act because icons were originally sacred images—"artistic" representations of Christ. Today, icons are much less sanctified, for twentieth-century Western society has *canonized,* somewhat indiscriminately, many persons high and low. Among the worthy, Wolfgang Amadeus Mozart, Johann Sebastian Bach, Vincent van Gogh, and Winston Churchill are all icons. But because today's icons are not beyond reproach, characters like Adolf Hitler, Richard Nixon, and Ronald Reagan are icons as well. These latter figures have become iconic for their "accomplishments," and hence have been imbued with symbolic attributes. Good or bad, each has become a paradigm of sorts: Bach for his genius, Hitler for his evil, and Reagan for his senility.

Iconic paintings and sculpture, like iconic personalities, are often used to humorous advantage, and certain historical styles also possess symbolic powers. When Seymour Chwast creat-

ed three hundred "portraits" of Bach to commemorate the composer's three-hundredth birthday in the book *Happy Birthday Bach,* the idea was to represent Bach during every year since his birth, including those long past his death. Bach was caricatured in the context of each particular year, usually in a style appropriately representative of the given period. In so doing, Chwast not only affectionately satirized Bach the icon, but also employed iconographic styles as recognizable signposts. Chwast used accessible historical references as comic backgrounds, adding another level of irony to the portrait.

The American flag flies high on the list of the world's most powerful symbols. Like all flags, it is a mnemonic device, but its simple design evokes complex, often contradictory responses—while it symbolizes freedom, liberty, and bounty, it simultaneously suggests military and economic power used for good and evil. As the ultimate symbol of America, it must remain various things

NOTHING IS MORE ICONIC THAN GOD,
BUT WHEN COMBINED WITH MONEY
("IN GOD WE TRUST"), THE MESSAGE
BECOMES A STRIDENT COMMENTARY,
AS IN THIS 1987 PIECE.
ART DIRECTOR/DESIGNER:
LUCY BARTHOLOMAY
CLIENT: THE BOSTON GLOBE

MICKEY MAO, FROM 1989'S THE 90'S: A
LOOK BACK SURGICALLY COMBINES TWO
WELL-KNOWN FIGURES.
ART DIRECTOR/DESIGNER: PAULA SCHER
COPYWRITER: TONY HENDRA
CLIENT: TONY HENDRA, AVON BOOKS

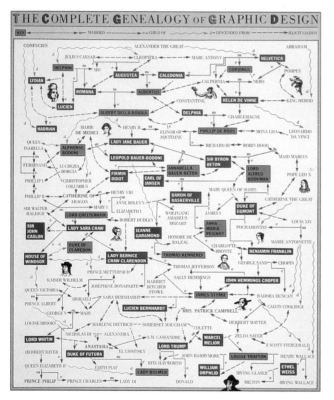

ABOVE: IN "THE COMPLETE
GENEALOGY OF GRAPHIC DESIGN,"
1985, PAULA SCHER PARODIES
GENEALOGY CHARTS AND POKES FUN
AT THE MOVERS AND SHAKERS OF
THIS PROFESSION.
DESIGNER: PAULA SCHER
CLIENT: PRINT MAGAZINE

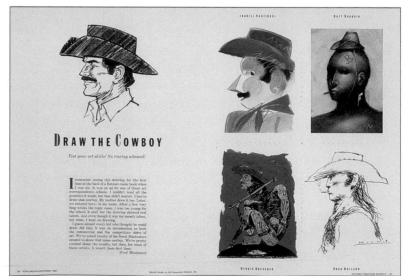

"DRAW THE COWBOY," FROM 1984,
ELEVATES MATCHBOOK ART TO
A HIGH PLANE.
DESIGNER: FRED WOODWARD
ILLUSTRATORS: VARIOUS
CLIENT: TEXAS MONTHLY

KIT HINRICHS'S 1989 <u>STARS AND STRIPES</u> BOOK COMBINES THE IDEAS OF ART AND FLAG.
ART DIRECTOR: KIT HINRICHS
DESIGNER: CHRIS HILL
CLIENT: CHRONICLE BOOKS

HAPPY BIRTHDAY BACH, PUBLISHED IN 1987, EXPLORES THREE HUNDRED YEARS OF THE COMPOSER'S LIFE AND SPIRIT.
DESIGNER/ILLUSTRATOR: SEYMOUR CHWAST
CLIENT: DOUBLEDAY INC.

BACH IN ALL HIS FINERY IS HERE TRANSFORMED INTO A CONTEMPORARY 1990 MAN.
DESIGNER: MILTON GLASER
CLIENT: TOMATO RECORDS

"MONA ARTIST" IS ONE OF THE PERENNIAL <u>MONA LISA</u> SEND-UPS.
ILLUSTRATOR: JAMES MARSH
CLIENT: ARTBANK

"THE NEWS OF FALL IN NEW YORK," FROM A 1974 ISSUE OF <u>NEW YORK</u>, GIVES NEW MEANING TO THE CLASSIC ADAM AND EVE POSE.
ART DIRECTOR: WALTER BERNARD
DESIGNER/ILLUSTRATOR: SEYMOUR CHWAST
CLIENT: <u>NEW YORK</u> MAGAZINE

Two Surprises for the Class

"Today the class will begin a new project," said Dick.

"Oh," said Tim.

"Oh," said Jill.

"Oh," said Matt.

"Oh," said Pam.

"I have two surprises," said Dick.

"Oh!" said the class.

16

The First Surprise

"The first surprise is this mouse," said Dick.

"That does not look like a mouse," said Tim.

"It is an Apple II mouse," said Dick.

"Can Puff play with this mouse?" asked Jill.

"No, but every mouse we have
will make our Apple IIs easier to use."

"See," said Dick, "this disk is called *Instant Pascal*."

"Now the screen looks like my big brother's
Macintosh™," said Jill.

"Yes!" said Dick. "It works the same way, too."

17

<u>DO MORE WITH DICK AND JANE</u> IS A 1986 SEND-UP ON A CHILDREN'S CLASSIC.
ART DIRECTORS: CLEMENT MOK, JILL SAVINI
DESIGNER: JILL SAVINI
CLIENT: APPLE COMPUTERS

to various people. Kit Hinrichs celebrated the flag in his book, *Stars & Stripes* (Chronicle, 1988), allowing 96 designers and illustrators the freedom to "redesign" Old Glory based on their own political or aesthetic motivations in any way they saw fit.

Predictably, many of the images are sardonic commentaries, while others are simply formal exercises; some are witty, others serious. Indeed, Chris Hill's design for the cover is a clever visual pun: The flag is composed of red, white, and blue pencil points, referring, of course, to the artists' interpretations inside.

Institutional icons are also tools (and targets) of the visual humorist. The institution of marriage, for instance, is often addressed, and while it may be stretching the term, there can be no institution more *human* (or indeed more iconic) than motherhood. Herb Lubalin's most memorable and endearing visual pun is the 1967 typographic treatment for the *Mother & Child* logo (see page 32), in which the ampersand and the word *Child* fit comfortably inside the *o* of *Mother*, with *Child* nestled in an identifiably fetal

position. Turning to a more illustrative approach, the 1976 issue 64 of the *Push Pin Graphic*, devoted to "Mothers," carried illustrations of the mothers of such famous artists as Giotto, Toulouse-Lautrec, Juan Gris, and Jackson Pollack, each skillfully rendered by Push Pin's illustrators in the manner of the sons' respective "mature" styles.

Icons can be made humorous in a variety of ways. Exaggeration and distortion, as in caricature, are the most common. But caricature is not just limited to public faces—Seymour Chwast's covers for *Design & Style*, for instance, are actually caricatures of historical art icons, in which he twists, distorts, and reinterprets the essence of old styles and places them in a contemporary context.

THE JOY OF PARODY Art is a process of making icons, sometimes even unintentionally, for freezing time, space, and even emotion into permanent form contributes to an icon's definition. Parody, meanwhile, is the "art" of imitating a serious subject in a nonsensical or ridiculous manner (but generally with underlying intent). The most striking art icons include da Vinci's *Mona Lisa*, Michelangelo's *David*, Picasso's *Les Demoiselles d'Avignon*, Magritte's *Ce n'est pas*

COULD ANYONE HAVE GUESSED THAT
EDDIE MURPHY'S NAME WAS SO
SIMILAR TO THE EVERLAST LOGO, AS
SEEN IN THIS 1988 GRAPHIC?
ART DIRECTOR: FRED WOODWARD
DESIGNER: GAIL ANDERSON
LETTERER: DENNIS ORTIZ-LOPEZ
CLIENT: ROLLING STONE

AIGA/NEW YORK'S 1989 SPEAKER
SCHEDULE IS BASED ON THE FRONT
PAGE OF THE NEW YORK POST.
DESIGNER: ANTHONY RUSSELL
CLIENT: AIGA/NEW YORK

EDDIEMURPHY

un Pipe, and, of course, Grant Wood's *American Gothic*. With the exception of *American Gothic*, which has earned more praise than it really deserves, these are undeniably great works of art that aesthetically transcend their respective places in time, and it should come as no surprise that some of the most recurring visual parodies are made of these works. Parody has made *American Gothic* such a charged symbol that *Life* magazine devoted a feature story to its various incarnations. Magritte's parodists (and copyists) are so numerous in editorial, advertising, and graphic design that a book-length examination of the of the phenomenon was published in France, with the ironic title *Ce n'est pas un Magritte*. Parodies of classic artworks range from witty reinvention to silly cliché, yet all are essentially visual puns, since they play on two or more applications of one image.

In recent years, historicism has influenced the work of contemporary graphic designers, leading to the development of a number of exclusively graphic design icons. Designs in the form of posters by the Russian Constructivists El Lissitzky and Alexander Rodchenko, the French posterist A. M. Cassandre, and the Swiss photomontagist Herbert Matter have either been quoted, parodied, or otherwise osmosed into the working language of Post-Modernism. While parody does serve an educative function, historical references presented to designers unaware of the originals' design contexts can also become an exclusive in-joke, especially if the references are too elitist or obscure.

Despite its recurrence as a method of graphic wit and design humor, parody is one of the most difficult methods to achieve successfully. If the parodist takes too many liberties, then the parody will suffer; conversely, if the material is not twisted enough, the result could read as mimicry, or, worse, plagiarism. If the object of the parody is not universally known—or is known only by a few members of the targeted audience—then, at best, the result might be an interesting design but not a successful parody. For example, Seymour Chwast proposed a poster to Pizza Hut, based on El Lissitzky's "well-known" "Beat the Whites with the Red Wedge" poster, showing a triangular wedge carved out of a cir-

NY TALK'S 1988 ANNIVERSARY ISSUE
MIMICS THE EMBLEMATIC BOX OF
TIDE DETERGENT.
DESIGNER: MARK MICHAELSON
CLIENT: NY TALK

BOTTOM: THIS 1985 POSTER DRAWS
ITS INSPIRATION FROM A TYPICAL
COVER OF THE NATIONAL ENQUIRER.
ART DIRECTOR: DIANA GILL
DESIGNER: MIKE HICKS
ILLUSTRATOR: MELINDA MANISCALCO
CLIENT: AIGA/TEXAS

RIGHT: THE DESIGNER OF THIS 1988
NEW YORK CITY MARATHON POSTER
FAVORS A WELL-KNOWN GREEK MOTIF
ALSO FOUND ON COFFEE CUPS IN
RESTAURANTS AROUND NEW YORK.
DESIGNER/ILLUSTRATOR: JAMES
MCMULLAN
CLIENT: NEW YORK CITY MARATHON

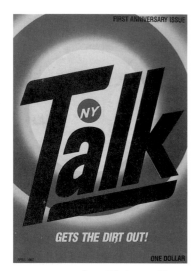

cle. As parody, it was also a witty pun, since the abstract geometry of Lissitzky's composition could indeed be seen as a slice of the pie. Unaware of the historical references, however, the client saw only an unacceptable design solution. Using the same reference, Pentagram/New York designed a brochure cover for Elektra Records in which Lissitzky's white circle was replaced by an LP record. Whether the client or the brochure's recipients understood the reference is unknown, but the piece was indeed published. Paula Scher's poster for Swatch Watches is a clever parody of one of Herbert Matter's most impressive late-1930s Swiss Tourist Board posters. Matter's photomontages were ubiquitous in Switzerland and are reproduced often in poster collections, but few recipients of the message would have understood the reference when Scher conceived her parody. Was it, therefore, unsuccessful? As a parody, yes, but it had the curious effect of introducing a generation of designers to the legacy of Matter, and perhaps even to Swiss design.

One of the most effective parodies of graphic design is Woody Pirtle's twist on Milton Glaser's Dylan poster, in which Bob Dylan's silhouetted profile is replaced by Glaser's distinctive visage. In place of the huge shock of rainbow-patterned hair that so brilliantly character-ized Dylan, Glaser's pate was emphasized by a receding rainbowed hairline. (Incidentally, Glaser's original design was based on a rare silhouetted self-profile drawn decades before by Marcel Duchamp—an homage of which most viewers are unaware.)

The most common design parodies, however, are not parodies of design icons but of books and magazines, requiring a graphic designer to adhere religiously to an original format (see interview with David Kaestle on page 143). Even a simple typeface alteration or a slight deviation from standard folio treatment can break the spell of this sort of parody. During the 1978 New York City newspaper strike, which completely shut down the three major dailies, a *New York Times* mysteriously appeared on the newsstands.

THIS 1985 SWATCH AD VIGOROUSLY
PARODIES HERBERT MATTER'S
WELL-KNOWN POSTER FOR THE
SWISS TOURIST BOARD.
DESIGNER: PAULA SCHER
CLIENT: SWATCH

"GLASER" IS A BRILLIANT 1986
SEND-UP OF GLASER'S OWN CLASSIC
"DYLAN" POSTER.
DESIGNER: WOODY PIRTLE
CLIENT: DALLAS SOCIETY OF VISUAL
COMMUNICATION

BELOW LEFT: THIS REACTOR 1989 AD
ECHOES THE ART OF STALINIST RUSSIA.
DESIGNER: LOUIS FISCHAUF
CLIENT: REACTOR

BELOW RIGHT: A SOVIET MAGAZINE, 1927.

BOTTOM: CURRENTS TAKES OFF ON
EL LISSITZKY'S ARCHETYPAL POSTER,
"BEAT THE WHITES WITH THE RED WEDGE."
DESIGNER: HAROLD BURCH, PENTAGRAM
CLIENT: ELEKTRA RECORDS

In fact, it was *Not The New York Times*, a parody so visually precise that it forced a double take. Of course, since New Yorkers were starved for news during the three-month strike, *Not The New York Times* was a hit, and not only for its brilliant parody of the *Times*—for those readers deprived of their daily newsprint "fix," it was like a synthetic substitute. A few years later, a parody of the *New York Times Book Review* failed to capture the visual and textual essence of the publication, reminding us that successful parody is never easy.

Not The New York Times was a direct parody of a major institution in the tradition of the *Harvard Lampoon* and later *National Lampoon,* but sometimes parodists, like body snatchers, will use the formats of well-known publications for *indirect* parody. Such was the case with *Dogue,* a 1987 send-up of *Vogue,* wherein chic canines were substituted for haute-coutured women. With this type of parody fidelity to the original design format is ostensibly irrelevant, since the host publication merely serves as a convenient vehicle.

These parodies were initiated by outsiders; when parody is done by insiders, it is called *self-parody,* and is sometimes more difficult to achieve, due to an overfamiliarity with the material. In 1985, *Print* magazine asked Paula Scher and me to write and design a parody issue of their publication. While the format was easy to parody, the content was difficult. Was the parody to be of the magazine itself (a confluence of diverse though related articles about design), without a common stylistic thread? Or was

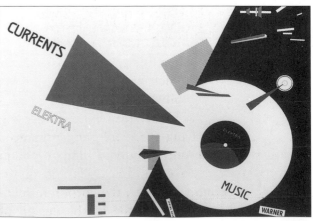

graphic design itself a better target for satire? The latter course, which was eventually chosen, offered many possibilities, including preposterous articles on how Walter Keane, the once-fashionable painter of big-eyed children, influenced American illustration; a fictional interview with Anale Retentiv, an orthodox Swiss designer; Renoir's lost commercial art; the corporate identity of Canada; and a profile of the design of Lubevitch & Moscowitz, famed "deli designers." It can be argued that this last article, playing off common deli and luncheonette waiter's checks, signboards, and menus, was not so preposterous as it initially seemed, and is, in fact, the basis for much of what we now refer to as vernacular design, directly related to some of M&Co.'s work for Restaurant Florent (see Chapter 6). In fact, an article satirizing regional design for this parody issue further emphasized this point by awarding first place in a design competition to a common traffic sign. Scher's *Print* cover may also have been influential on the current trend in absurd information design—her illustration, a send-up of a family tree, predates similar applications in *Spy* magazine.

FAMILIARITY BREEDS AND BREEDS

Mark Twain said "Familiarity breeds contempt—and children," which may be only partly true about human relations but is all too true when referring to graphic design and illustration. Moreover, graphic wit and design humor suffer most from overuse. Shakespeare, presaging the problems caused by design competitions that publicize the best of the new and thereby give common currency to uncommon ideas, wrote, "Sweets grown common lose their dear delight." Though design humor must touch the chord of recognition to be effective, it still must be surprising. Familiar cues are necessary, but an overdose of any one conceit, trick, or otherwise wonderful idea can kill wit. And so, to draw upon a variation of that familiar bromide one last time, "Though familiarity may not breed contempt, it takes the edge off of admiration."

GRAFFITO CHRISTMAS INVITATION, 1989
ART DIRECTOR: TIM THOMPSON
DESIGNERS: MORTON JACKSON, JOE
PARISI, DAVE PLUNKERT
ILLUSTRATOR: DAVE PLUNKERT
PHOTOGRAPHER: MORTON JACKSON
CLIENT: GRAFFITO

JUMBLED LETTERS The ransom-note school of graphic design dates back to the nineteenth century, when job printers carelessly mixed disparate styles of wood type together on the same poster or bill, resulting in an anarchic visual effect. This emblematic Victorian typography was born as much of necessity (printers did not always have complete fonts on hand, and so were forced to use what was available) as of an intent to purposefully achieve visual exuberance. Since urban streets and boulevards were becoming increasingly cluttered with posters and advertisements in the late 1800s, it should come as no surprise that printers went through typographic contortions to attain novel, witty, and eye-catching prominence. While elegance is its own reward, raucousness (even anarchy) has certain virtues too, particularly when the purpose is to capture and hold a reader, viewer, or customer. In any design period, designers with high levels of aesthetic consciousness will always strive for balance, harmony, and, of course, legibility, yet just as often there will be renegades to enliven (or degrade) the printed page, often by breaking typographic rules. Though not the first and certainly not the last, the Italian Futurists and German Dadaists targeted the nineteenth century's canon of legibility as a symbol of old-fogeyism. Vanguard Futurist and Dadaist typographic designers violently dismantled theretofore accepted standards by producing hysterical type that was not simply a metaphor for the new order but the archetype of a distinctly new visual language.

The jumbled letter compositions shown in this section descend from various art-historical

BELOW: MUSIC, DANCE HEADLINE/
DISPLAY TYPE, 1989
DESIGNER: ALEX ISLEY
CLIENT: BROOKLYN ACADEMY OF MUSIC

FACING PAGE, BOTTOM: "GAG REFLEX"
MAGAZINE ARTICLE OPENER, 1989
ART DIRECTOR: FRED WOODWARD
DESIGNERS: GAIL ANDERSON,
DEBRA BISHOP
ILLUSTRATOR: STEVEN GUARNACCIA
CLIENT: ROLLING STONE

AZ YOU LIKE IT TYPE FOUNDRY CHART, 1989
DESIGNERS: RICHARDSON OR RICHARDSON
CLIENT: SELF

sources, including Victorian, Dada, and Surrealism; more to the point, they are inspired by comics and comic books, bad job printing, and, of course, those clichéd ransom notes that Ray Elliot of Bob and Ray referred to in one of their classic comic routines as having too many *san sareefs*. Funny letters can be handmade (drawn or drafted) somewhat randomly, without regard for uniformity, or they can be bastardized versions of real type, essentially cut and pasted for heightened comic results. But whatever the medium, the intent is to throw the eye off balance, and so too the equilibrium.

FUNNY FACES Goudy Stout is not a syrupy malt beverage but a rare, quirky typeface designed in 1930 by America's leading type designer, Frederic W. Goudy, One step above comic book lettering, it has only one true positive attribute: Its *A* seems to be based on the comic gait of Charlie Chaplin's famed Little Tramp. "In a moment of typographic weakness," Goudy later wrote, "I attempted to produce a 'black' letter

that would interest those advertisers who like the bizarre in their print." Although he might protest otherwise, the requisites of the advertising business were clear when he made this minor folly; attention in the growing marketplace was not going to be wrested by elegant or classic typefaces, but by eye-catching combinations of letterform and image. The odder the letter, the better.

"HOT" MAGAZINE ARTICLE OPENER, 1989
ART DIRECTOR: FRED WOODWARD
DESIGNERS: FRED WOODWARD,
GAIL ANDERSON
CLIENT: ROLLING STONE

RIGHT: "GEEK LOVE" BOOK TITLE TYPE
TREATMENT, 1989
ART DIRECTOR: CAROL CARSON
DESIGNER: CHIP KIDD
CLIENT: ALFRED A. KNOPF

GEEK LOVE

Funny or novelty letterforms and typefaces, many from bygone eras, were therefore called to action in the competitive war to win consumer attention. In fact, many respected type designers added their own weird types to a growing library of faces used for everything from leaflets to billboards.

One should not, however, ascribe this to the "when bad type happens to good designers" syndrome. Some of these novelty faces are actually quite beautiful (e.g., A. M. Cassandre's *Bifur* and Morris Fuller Benton's *Broadway*), and many more are truly humorous, or are at least used in humorous contexts. Novelty typefaces have an interesting history dating back to the early nineteenth century, owing to the Industrial Revolution and the subsequent development of commerce. In *Printing Types: An Introduction* (Beacon Press, 1971), Alexander Lawson writes that the new typographic fashion began in the early 1800s, when English typefounders produced "a variety of embellished types designed to emphasize their unique characteristics for the single purpose of attracting attention. Fat faces, grotesques, and Egyptians—decorative types when compared to the romans, which had undergone minor changes since the Italian fifteenth century—were not flamboyant enough for the new requirements of advertising display." This sparked furious competition among typefounders to outdo each other in the production of ornamented and fancy faces. One of the most well-known fancy faces, called Rustic in England or Log Cabin in the United States, was designed at the Vincent Figgins Foundry in 1845 and is still in currency today, albeit certainly not for body text and only for limited appropriate uses (like public signage).

The fashion for ornamented, fancy, and novelty faces comes and goes. Recently, however, some vintage specimens have been revived to give an explicitly humorous edge to contemporary visual communications. Semiotically speaking, Log Cabin is perfect for imparting the idea of the great outdoors. Liariat, and its variant, Roy Rogers Bold, unambiguously signal a Western theme. A revived 1930s trifle called Vulcan suggests the motion and speed of that streamlined era, while Howard Trafton's Cartoon, a brush letter that looks as it sounds, is ubiquitous in 1950s retro design. And Milton Glaser's Baby Teeth, derived from a popular Italian Art Deco alphabet, while it may not look like any human

EVERY YEAR WE ATTEMPT TO DISCERN WHAT IS HOT. IT'S A SOMEWHAT ABSURD JOB, SINCE THE WORD "HOT" IS NEARLY IMPOSSIBLE TO DEFINE OBJECTIVELY. THIS YEAR, HOWEVER, THERE DOES SEEM TO BE ONE SPECIFIC, AND RATHER CONTRADICTORY, GENERAL TREND: AMBIVALENCE MIXED WITH COMFORT. MEANING, NO ONE WANTS TO COMMIT TO ANYTHING, BUT EVERYONE STILL LONGS TO BE IN WONDERFUL SURROUNDINGS WHILE CONSIDERING HIS OPTIONS. THESE DAYS ARE MARKED BY ADORABLE PUPPIES AND CONVENIENT ALIBIS, BY BEAUTIFUL WALLPAPER AND HANDY EXCUSES. THE GOAL OF THIS ISSUE, HOWEVER, IS TO BE UNAMBIVALENT. WHAT WE'RE ATTEMPTING IS NOT ONLY TO TAKE STOCK OF THE PRESENT AND PREDICT THE FUTURE BUT TO EXPLAIN HOW HOT HAPPENS AND WHAT ITS EFFECTS ARE. SOME OF OUR CHOICES MAY SEEM STRANGE, OTHERS OBVIOUS, BUT THE PURPOSE IS NOT SO MUCH TO ENDORSE AS TO INFORM. AFTER ALL, WE WANT YOU TO MAKE UP YOUR OWN MIND. • • •

Guest Editor LYNN HIRSCHBERG

BODY OF OPINION BOOK COVER
ART DIRECTOR: FRANK METZ
DESIGNER: MARK FISHER
CLIENT: SUMMIT BOOKS

FOUND ALPHABET, 1977
DESIGNER: MERVYN KURLANSKY,
PENTAGRAM
CLIENT: PRESTON POLYTECHNIC

LUST BOOK COVER, 1989
ART DIRECTOR: SARA EISENMAN
DESIGNER: CARIN GOLDBERG,
CARIN GOLDBERG GRAPHIC DESIGN
CLIENT: HOUGHTON MIFFLIN

BOTTOM: BOTANY TIE
ADVERTISEMENT, 1938
DESIGNER: UNKNOWN

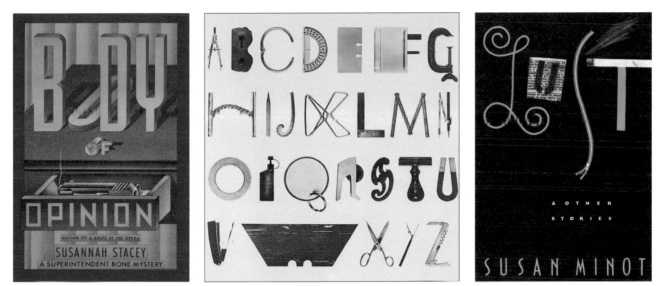

bicuspids, is a spirited design signaling a basic lightheartedness.

The number of funny faces far exceeds the capacity of this book if one includes the multitude of expressive novelty faces that were stylized period types and have, with time, become inherently humorous due to changes in fashion. (For a comprehensive showing, Dover Books offers a vast array, as do the various out-of-print type-specimen books available at flea markets and second-hand book emporia.) Shown here is but a small sampling of the short-lived, long-lasting, and current attempts at achieving typographic comedy.

METAMORPHIC LETTERING If the Trajan inscription is the paradigm of Roman letterforms, then the Gellone *Sacramentarium*, dating from between 755 and 787 A.D., is perhaps the archetype of metamorphic, even comic, lettering. This ancient document is one of the finest exam-

ples of how illuminators transformed figures of man and beast into individual letters, a practice that ultimately led to the development of printing and beyond. In ancient times, metamorphic letters also served as sacred metaphors and allegories, communicating either complex tales or simple messages. Playing off the relationship of, say, an object to a letterform, typographic metamorphosis can also be a form of visual punning,

SIN CITY ALPHABET, 1983
ART DIRECTOR: STEVEN HELLER
ILLUSTRATOR: STEVEN GUARNACCIA
CLIENT: A&W PUBLICATIONS

BOTTOM LEFT: ALPHABET OF BUGS, 1974
ART DIRECTOR: ANDREW KNER
ILLUSTRATOR: ISTVÁN DROSZ
CLIENT: PRINT MAGAZINE

BOTTOM RIGHT: SPD CALL FOR
ENTRIES, 1990
DESIGNER: FRED WOODWARD
CLIENT: THE SOCIETY OF
PUBLICATION DESIGNERS

"STRAVINSKY" TELEVISION DOCU-
MENTARY PROPOSAL COVER, 1979
DESIGNER: TOM SUMIDA
CLIENT: WGBH BOSTON

BOTTOM: RESTAURANT FLORENT
"MIRTH" POSTCARD, 1989
ART DIRECTOR: TIBOR KALMAN
DESIGNER: MARLENE MCCARTY
CLIENT: RESTAURANT FLORENT

as in the Society of Publication Designers's call-for-entry poster, in which three French curves form the initials *SPD*.

RAP TYPOGRAPHY Milton Glaser once said, "Young artists must make their own discoveries, even if they are old discoveries"; the Bible says there is nothing new under the sun. Therefore, designers currently engaged in the practice of distorting, contorting, and otherwise exorting type to approximate sound or sound bites are not doing anything that hasn't already been done by their elders or betters. Type learned to speak centuries ago, and was given dialects the instant more than one variation of the Roman alphabet was developed. Each type family includes a unique voice, with the variations within that family functioning like regional accents. As the primary means of communication for centuries, type has extraordinary powers that are often taken for granted.

"Words," wrote the British novelist Somerset Maugham, "have weight, sound and appearance. Words make sentences. And type makes those sentences good to look at and good to listen to." Lewis Carroll knew of this power when he had his typesetter concretize certain passages in *Alice in Wonderland,* just as Guillaume Apollinaire understood when he devised his first *Calligrammes.*

Talking type, while virtually as old as type itself, is never old hat. Accents may change from culture to culture, volume may be modulated from project to project, but type continues to speak at all levels. The Futurists' and Dadaists' typographic voices were loud, the Aestheticists' were quiet. With so many accents, dialects, and styles from which to choose, it is no wonder the contemporary murmur of typographic babble is getting louder. Paul Rand refers to the latest manifestation of talking type as *rap typography,* literally suggesting the syncopation, rhythm, and rhyme found in rap music. However, Rand means that today's talking type can be improvisational like jazz, varied like a partita, or structured like a motet—expressive at best, nihilistic at worst.

Rap typography is not exclusively concerned with the approximation of sound, but takes many forms from onomatopoeic poems (à la Marinetti's *parole in liberta*) to the transparent and layered typographics referred to in today's design argot as "deconstruction." The sources of rap typography vary, and the technique cannot be pigeonholed merely as a humorous or stylistic conceit, though much of what is current *is* stylistic. Some designers are truly experimenting with relationships of form and meaning; others are

"Can You Say Rebound?" Nike
advertisement, 1990
Art Director/Designer:
Michael Prieve
Creative Directors: Dan Weiden,
David Kennedy
Agency: Weiden & Kennedy
Photographer: Jose Picayo
Copywriter: Jim Riswold
Client: Nike
Reprinted by permission of Nike

Neighborhood Dilemma album
cover, 1990
Art Director/Designer:
Tom Bonauro
Photographer: Jeffery Newbury
Client: Tripindicular Records

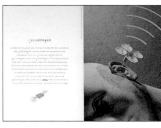

Above: Productolith
brochure, 1988
Concept and Design:
Rick Valicenti/Thirst
Concept and Outline:
Gib Marquardt
Photography: Tom Vack
and Corinne Pfister
Typography: Tardis
Typography
Client: Consolidated Paper

Left: Lisa Ramezzano
business card, 1989
Designer: Michael Mabry
Client: Lisa Ramezzano,
Casting Agent.

WATCHING THE BODY BURN BOOK
COVER, 1990
ART DIRECTOR/DESIGNER: CHIP KIDD
CLIENT: ALFRED A. KNOPF

FACING PAGE, BOTTOM RIGHT: MTV
MUSIC AWARDS CD COVER, 1990
ART DIRECTOR/DESIGNER:
GIANNI DONN
COPYWRITER: SHARON GLASSMAN
CLIENT: MTV NETWORKS

"WAS IST DADA?" PERIODICAL, 1921
DESIGNER: KURT SCHWITERS

SQUABBLE BOOK JACKET, 1990
ART DIRECTOR: SARA EISENMAN
DESIGNER: CARIN GOLDBERG,
CARIN GOLDBERG DESIGN
CLIENT: HOUGHTON MIFFLIN

FETISH COVER, 1979
ART DIRECTOR/DESIGNERS: JANE
KOSSTRIN, DAVID STERLING,
TERENCE MAIN
FIRM: DOUBLESPACE
PHOTOGRAPHER: RIK SFERRA
CLIENT: FETISH, A SELF-PUBLISHED
MAGAZINE

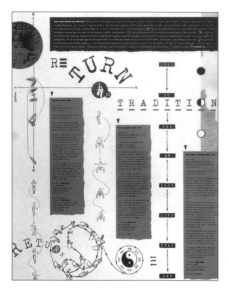

just perpetuating a code. Recent advertisements for Nike shown here represent a synthesis of these two approaches into what has quickly become a popular typographic style, at once eye-catching and witty. Indeed, these ads and other manifestations indicate a type-as-art revival in youth-targeted advertising today.

TYPE FACES Bradbury Thompson devotes a chapter of his book, *The Art of Graphic Design,* to "Type as Toy," which he defines as "graphic design conceived in the spirit of play and a sentiment for childhood." There can be no more obvious return to child's play in graphic design than the making of faces from type and letterforms. These are puns in the truest sense, as they are substitutions of one form for another—in this case, the appropriate letter for a mouth, an ear, a nose, or hair. The practice dates back to the development of letterforms and is an efficient mnemonic device, for it speaks simultaneously in language and in symbol.

"JCH" LOGO, 1988
ART DIRECTORS: TAKAAKI
MATSUMOTO, MICHAEL MCGUINN,
M PLUS M INC.
DESIGNER: MICHAEL MCGINN
CLIENT: JCH GROUP LTD.

"SOLO" LOGO, 1990
ART DIRECTOR: SEYMOUR CHWAST
DESIGNER: GREG SIMPSON
CLIENT: SOLO EDITIONS

THE 90S BOOK COVER, 1989
ART DIRECTOR/DESIGNER:
PAULA SCHER
CLIENT: TONY
HENDRA/AVON BOOKS

"CG SHOW" INVITATION, 1989
DESIGNER: ALEXANDER ISLEY
CLIENT: AIGA/NEW YORK

DAVID BOWIE LOGO, 1989
DESIGNER: LAURIE ROSENWALD
CLIENT: PENABAKER PRODUCTIONS

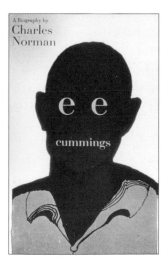

"ROBOT" ADVERTISEMENT,
1986
DESIGNER/ILLUSTRATOR:
TOM GEISMAR
CLIENT: SIMPSON PAPER CO.

"THE JOYS OF TOYS" EXHIBITION
POSTER, 1989
ART DIRECTOR: CHRIS HILL
DESIGNER: DAVID LERCH
CLIENT: THE GALLERIA/GERALD D.
HINES INTERESTS

E.E. CUMMINGS BOOK JACKET, 1967
DESIGNER: MILTON GLASER
CLIENT: SIGNET BOOKS

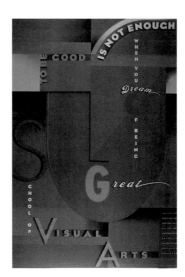

"MOVED" POSTER, 1989
ART DIRECTORS: TAKAAKI
MATSUMOTO, MICHAEL
McGINN, M PLUS M INC.
DESIGNER: MICHAEL McGINN
CLIENT: JCH GROUP LTD.

ZOTOS FUNNY FACE
LOGO, 1989
DESIGNER: RICK
VALICENTI/THIRST
CLIENT: SHISEIDO

"LO" LOGO, 1988
DESIGNER: RICK
VALICENTI/ THIRST
CLIENT: LYRIC OPERA
OF CHICAGO

M&M CHRISTMAS CARD, 1989
ART DIRECTOR: RON SULLIVAN
DESIGNER: JOHN FLAMING/
SULLIVAN PERKINS
CLIENT: SELF

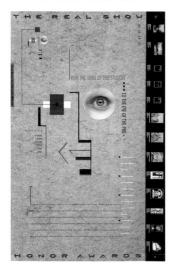

"THE REAL SHOW" POSTER, 1988
ART DIRECTOR/DESIGNER/
ILLUSTRATOR: DAVID PLUNKERT,
GRAFFITO, INC.
PHOTOGRAPHER: LIGHTSTRUCK STUDIO
CLIENT: ART DIRECTOR'S CLUB OF
METROPOLITAN WASHINGTON, D.C.

"TO BE GOOD IS NOT ENOUGH"
POSTER, 1987
ART DIRECTORS: SILAS RHODES,
PAULA SCHER
DESIGNER: PAULA SCHER
CLIENT: THE SCHOOL OF VISUAL ARTS

"POSTSCRIPT IMPROVED MY LOOKS"
ADVERTISEMENT, 1991
ART DIRECTOR: MARTY NEUMEIR
COPYWRITERS: CHRISTOPHER CHU,
LES CHIBANA
CLIENT: ADOBE SYSTEMS, INC.

"SAVE THE WAILS" POSTER, 1985
ART DIRECTOR/DESIGNER:
JOHN MULLER
WRITER: JOHN MULLER
CLIENT: KANSAS CITY JAZZ
COMMISSION

"CONVERSIONS" TYPOGRAPHER
ADVERTISEMENT, 1988
ART DIRECTOR: DAVID BARTELS,
BARTELS & CARSTENS
ILLUSTRATOR: BILL VUKSANOVICH
COPYWRITER: DON CARSTENS
CLIENT: MASTER TYPOGRAPHERS

"HE KILLS ME" POSTER, 1989
DESIGNER: DONALD MOFFETT
CLIENT: ART/STREET PROJECTS

"PORK" POSTER, 1989
DESIGNER: DONALD MOFFETT
CLIENT: ART/STREET PROJECTS

WORDPLAY   Typography gives words texture, even allure, but make no mistake about it—without the right words, there can be no meaning. Similarly, rap music may be entertaining, but it is at its best when the lyrics conjure up meaningful mental pictures. And rhyme without content is like doo-wop—toe-tapping, knee-slapping, but soon tiresome. Although this book's introduction began with a discussion of graphic design as the marriage of word and image, most of the examples shown here lean toward visual solutions in which words are secondary, if used at all. This section brings graphic wit and design humor back full-circle to the word as the focus. In most cases, the design is secondary to the humorous headline and slogan. Nevertheless, these works offer a harmonious mix of type, image, and word.

"SIT" PROGRAM FOR AIGA
CONFERENCE, 1989
DESIGNER: JACK SUMMERFORD
WRITER: JACK SUMMERFORD
CLIENT: AIGA NATIONAL
CONFERENCE/SAN ANTONIO

"SAVE TWO BUCKS" HERBICIDE
ADVERTISEMENT, 1988
ART DIRECTOR: RON LOPEZ
DESIGNER: DAVID BARTELS,
BARTELS & CARSTENS
ILLUSTRATOR: ALEX MURAWSKI
COPYWRITER: DON CARSTENS
CLIENT: MONSANTO

NEW YORK POST "3 BIGGEST LIES"
AD CAMPAIGN, 1990
CREATIVE DIRECTOR: RICHARD
KIRSHENBAUM
ART DIRECTOR/DESIGNER:
BILL OBERLANDER
COPYWRITER: DAVID BUCKINGHAM
AGENCY: KIRSHENBAUM & BOND
CLIENT: THE NEW YORK POST

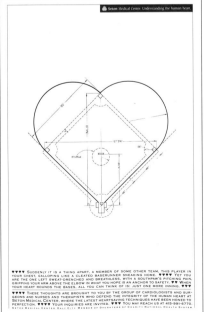

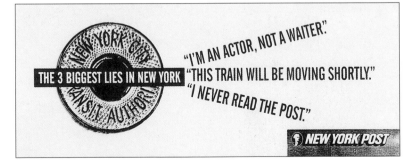

LEFT: "LOVE AND HEART" AD
CREATIVE DIRECTORS: BOB MANLEY,
DAN ALTMAN
ART DIRECTOR/DESIGNER:
BRENT CROXTON, ALTMAN AND
MANLEY COPYWRITERS: DAN ALTMAN,
CHIORI SANTIAGO
CLIENT: SETON MEDICAL CENTER

"SPACE MEN" BILLBOARD AD, 1988
ART DIRECTOR: JOHN SEYMOUR-
ANDERSON, MCCOOL & CO.
COPYWRITER: MIKE GIBBS
CLIENT: STEINER DEVELOPMENT

SPACE MEN SEEK CONTACT WITH LOCAL BUSINESS LEADERS.

STEINER DEVELOPMENT 473-5650

"WRONG WAY" INFORMATION-DESIGN
SEMINAR ANNOUNCEMENT, 1986
DESIGNER: CHRIS PULLMAN
COPYWRITER: CHRIS PULLMAN
CLIENT: AIGA/BOSTON

"WOULD YOU RATHER BE IN THEIR
SHOES?" SHOE ADVERTISEMENT, 1989
ART DIRECTOR/DESIGNER:
JOHN FOLLIS
COPYWRITER: RICHARD
KIRSCHENBAUM
AGENCY: KIRSHENBAUM & BOND
CLIENT: KENNETH COLE SHOES

"DON'T FORGET TO BRUSH" POSTER,
1988
ART DIRECTOR/COPYWRITER:
JOHN GREEN
AGENCY: BAUERLEIN
CLIENT: NEW ORLEANS DENTAL
SOCIETY

6 COMIC BUILDUP

DIAGRAMMING COMEDY Groucho Marx told Max Eastman that if Eastman could provide a test by which a good joke could be distinguished from a bad one without trying them out on the public, he would soon be the richest man in Hollywood. That said, he also predicted that Eastman would die poor. Indeed, such a goal was admittedly a good deal beyond Eastman's stated ambition "to educate the jokers of Hollywood"; rather, Eastman's mission in writing *The Enjoyment of Laughter* was to teach the public how to enjoy jokes whenever possible, to create "a handbook in comic pleasure." Likewise, the intent of this book is not to be so presumptuous as to instruct anyone in the art of being funny, but to survey those works that are truly witty and humorous, and to offer some context in which they might be appreciated. We stated at the beginning that overanalyzing humor is a sure way to bring about its downfall, and Eastman said that too. Yet despite his cautionary statements, he did endeavor to diagram a joke, which, he said, "might conceivably be of use to a humorist or a comedian . . . [or] at least be of use to the critics of humor." This book has used Eastman as a model and guide when possible, yet here it must part company—it is not possible to diagram graphic wit and design humor. But there *are* a few textbook cases that might prove instructive. In these well-planned strategies, wit and humor sneak up and deliver.

NEW ORLEANS DENTAL ASSOCIATION

Dentists are known for high rates of depression and suicide, but definitely not for great senses of humor. In fact, the funniest of my dental sessions

It's Not Too Late To Go Straight. More adults are wearing braces than ever before. New advances in orthodontic dentistry have made braces more comfortable and less obvious, often using special materials that match tooth color in place of metal bands. If you're ready to go straight, talk with your dentist. He just might give you something to really smile about. **New Orleans Dental Association**

Ignore Your Teeth, And Just See How They Come Out. Your teeth were meant to last a lifetime. But only if you take care of them. It still takes a thorough program of preventive hygiene. So see your dentist regularly, and don't forget to brush and floss. Because we'd rather see your smile come out ahead than come out of your head. **New Orleans Dental Association.**

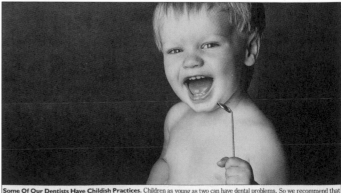

Some Of Our Dentists Have Childish Practices. Children as young as two can have dental problems. So we recommend that children visit a dentist before their third birthday. It'll help them grow up with a healthy attitude towards dentists and dental hygiene. And you'll see it every time they smile. Talk to your dentist for more information. **New Orleans Dental Association.**

New Orleans Dental Association, 1988
Creative Director/Art Director:
John Green
Photographers: Mike Terranova,
Lee Crum
Copywriter: Chris Sonnenberg
Agency: Bauerlein Inc.
Client: New Orleans Dental
Association

Forget To Floss, And You Might Have Just One Thing Left To Worry About. There's more to good dental hygiene than just brushing. It's important to floss, too, because tooth decay can be caused by bacteria *between* your teeth. So, please see your dentist regularly, and follow his advice. Because your teeth are important. Every last one of them. **New Orleans Dental Association.**

occurred when, while being taught how to floss, the demonstration false teeth flew out of the dentist's hands, out the window, and into a shopping cart below. The creatives at Bauerlein Inc. realized that unhealthy teeth are no laughing matter, that the old cautions were going unheeded, and, perhaps most of all, that dentists needed a witty and acerbic means of sending their messages. The 1988 campaign for the New Orleans Dental Association is a masterpiece of word- and picture play, simply and elegantly designed to grab the viewer and send him or her running off to that six-month cleaning.

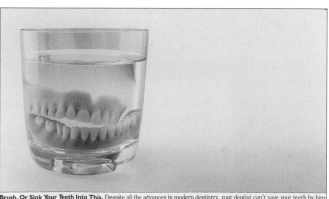

Brush. Or Sink Your Teeth Into This. Despite all the advances in modern dentistry, your dentist can't save your teeth by himself. It still takes your help, plus a regular and thorough program of preventive hygiene. So see your dentist, and follow his advice. Working together, you can keep your teeth from being in a glass by themselves. **New Orleans Dental Association**

LOUIS, BOSTON AD CAMPAIGN, 1990
ART DIRECTOR/DESIGNER: TYLER SMITH
COPY: GEOFF CURRIER
CLIENT: LOUIS, BOSTON

IF WE TOLD YOU ONCE, WE TOLD YOU XIV TIMES, THE NAME IS LOUIS—ECLECTIC CLOTHING FOR MEN AND WOMEN.

ECLECTIC CLOTHING FOR MEN AND WOMEN, NOT FOR THE AVERAGE JOE.

LOUIS, BOSTON When Louis, Boston, a hip clothing emporium headquartered in its namesake city, opened a New York store in 1990, it quickly blitzed the market with advertising in an effort to gain a foothold in the city's glut of haberdashers. In a series of memorable ads, Tyler Smith found an eye-catching and memorable way to get the name across and at the same time establish Louis, Boston's image as a creative hot spot, taking three famous Louis's—the fighter, the king, and the song by the Kingsmen.

JUST FOR THE RECORD, IT'S LOUIS, BOSTON—ECLECTIC CLOTHING FOR MEN AND WOMEN.

Each ad was similarly designed, but the images were sufficiently varied to demand attention each time. A verbal pun as a caption ("Just for the Record, It's Louis, Boston—Eclectic Clothing for Men and Women") helped clarify the rather difficult yet decidedly distinctive typographic band containing the store's name and address.

But even the wittiest advertising campaign is no match for the vicissitudes of a depressed economy, and in 1991, Louis, Boston closed the doors of its New York outlet.

MISSION SHOPPING CENTER
AD CAMPAIGN, 1989
ART DIRECTOR: JOHN MULLER
DESIGNERS: JOHN MULLER,
KENT MULKEY
WRITER: JOHN KRUEGER
CLIENT: COPAKEN WHITE BLITT

MISSION SHOPPING CENTER As teasers for the 1989 grand opening of the new Mission Shopping Center in Kansas City, John Muller pressed into service the images of a cast of television icons used to warm up the waiting consumer hordes. He transformed the entertainment giants into powerful graphic images by making them into high-contrast images, applying loud, flat colors to their faces, and gave each a pair of glasses made of watches—an allusion to grand opening time. Each poster also had a discreet pun for the headline—"We know best, we'll be opening any time now" over Robert Young of *Father Knows Best* fame, and "You'll be having a ball in no time, we're opening soon" above Lucille Ball's unmistakable visage.

RESTAURANT FLORENT AD CAMPAIGN,
1987–1990
ART DIRECTOR: TIBOR KALMAN, M&CO.
DESIGNERS: TIM HORN, ALEXANDER
ISLEY, BETHANY JOHNS, DEAN
LUBENSKY, MARLENE MCCARTY,
TIBOR KALMAN, M&CO.
CLIENT: RESTAURANT FLORENT

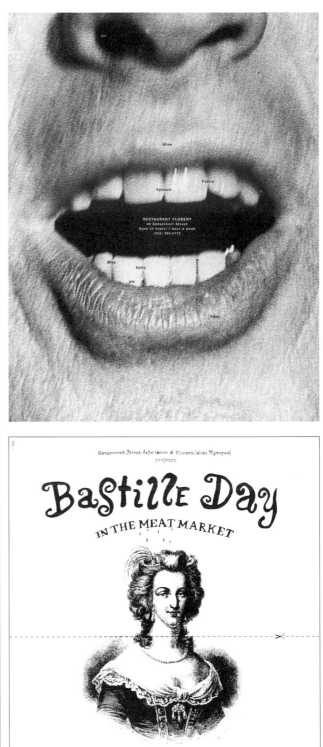

RESTAURANT FLORENT "Expect the unexpected" is the best way to describe M&Co.'s approach to the identity and ad campaigns launched in 1987 for Restaurant Florent, a chic eatery in New York's unsavory Gansevoort meat-packing district. The graphics are based on a pickup aesthetic—much of the imagery used for business cards, menus, matchbooks, and so on is from stock-art sources. The typography is comparatively simple and, therefore, inexpensive. And with the exception of the overall vernacular sensibility, the materials are visually inconsistent—indeed, some of the ads (which appear primarily in New York's *Paper*, a monthly downtown culture journal) are absurd. Take, for example, the larger-than-life open mouth showing stains and food particles on and in between glistening teeth. Other ads have social or political import, such as "Hunger," showing a plate and bone, with one address telling where to give food to the homeless and another telling where to come to eat (Restaurant Florent, of course). The ads have provided a unique identity for the restaurant, and at the same time are paradigms for a new genre of similarly absurdist campaigns.

WESTERN COFFEE SHOP T-SHIRTS, 1988
DESIGNER: ART CHANTRY
ILLUSTRATOR: MARK ZINGARELLI
CLIENT: WESTERN COFFEE SHOP

WESTERN COFFEE SHOP Art Chantry is known for smart, low-budget design solutions. To advertise Seattle's Western Coffee Shop in 1989, he created a series of low-cost T-shirt logos based on nostalgic themes that established the eatery as the best place to go for "Intense" espresso and meat-loaf sandwiches.

J&B AD CAMPAIGN, 1987-1990
CREATIVE DIRECTOR: ROY GRACE
ART DIRECTORS/DESIGNERS:
ROY GRACE, CHRIS GRAVES
COPYWRITERS: DAVID GORR, GRAIS
DEMETRE, DIANE ROTHCHILD
AGENCY: GRACE ROTHCHILD
CLIENT: J&B

J&B on the rocks.

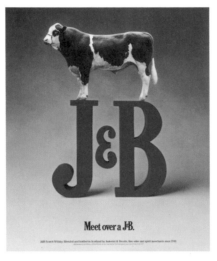

Meet over a J&B.

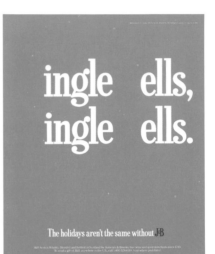

ingle ells,
ingle ells.

The holidays aren't the same without J&B

J&B It's not easy to make a whisky funny, but Grace Rothchild advertising did it the hard way, using a series of strained puns in clever contexts, in a campaign that began in 1988 and is still going strong as of this writing: "Meet over a J&B" shows a cow (meat) standing atop the J&B logo; "J&B at Home" shows an aerial view of a baseball park with, you guessed it, J&B at home plate; "J&B on the Rocks" lives up to its caption in the most obvious of ways; "J&B Neat" has the recognizable letterforms amongst a very sloppily hand-painted alphabet. Despite (indeed, *because of*), the obvious puns, the campaign succeeds in making the initials *J & B* memorable.

J&B neat.

J&B at home.

Absolut ad campaign, 1980–1990
Creative Directors: Arnie Arlow
and Peter Lubalin
Agency: TBWA

ABSOLUT L.A.

ABSOLUT PEAK.

ABSOLUT SEASON.

ABSOLUT LIMELIGHT.

ABSOLUT The most memorable of today's liquor ads is the ongoing campaign begun in 1980 by TBWA for Absolut Vodka, a textbook case of a patient advertiser allowing its campaign to build momentum. What began with a simple ad showing the elegant product package and the tagline "Absolut" developed into a collection of superb puns in which the Absolut bottle was vari-ously transformed by famous artists and photographers into a Christmas tree, a swimming pool, a golf course, and a ski slope. The ads' tag lines also evolved into single-line puns that have impact and memo-rability even with-out the accompa-nying images.

ABSOLUT ATTRACTION.

NIKE AD CAMPAIGN, 1989–1990
ART DIRECTOR/DESIGNER:
MICHAEL PRIEVE
PHOTOGRAPHERS: PETE STONE,
GARY NOLTON, DOUG PETTY
AGENCY: WEIDEN & KENNEDY
CLIENT: NIKE
REPRINTED BY PERMISSION FROM NIKE
(SABER-TOOTH CAT SKELETON
REPRINTED BY PERMISSION FROM
UNIVERSITY OF OREGON MUSEUM
OF NATURAL HISTORY)

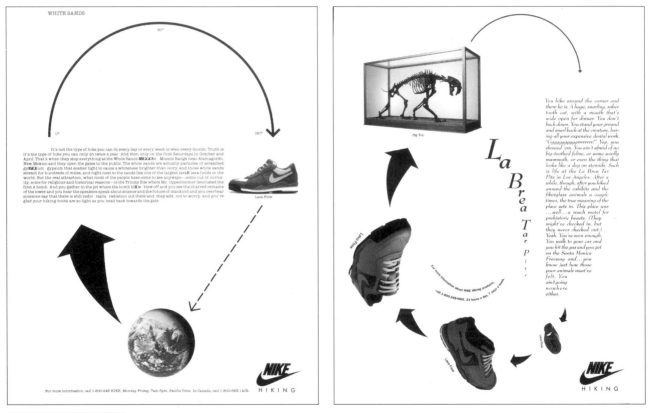

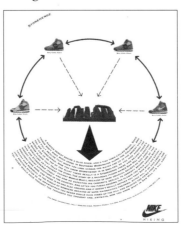

NIKE HIKING Nike has been on a roll ever since 1980, when the firm erected large billboards showing athletes at rest and work, with only the Nike logo as an identifier. Since then, the ads have gotten better and better, and in some cases funnier and funnier. The campaign for Nike Hiking devised by Weiden and Kennedy is not sidesplitting but *is* intellectual—it looks good and it takes a little time to get the full brunt of the humor. Eventually, the ad becomes so elegantly witty in both concept and execution that the series can't help but grab attention and ensure memorability. Each ad is based on a take-off of an informational graphic in which the Hiking shoes are related to Stonehenge, the La Brea Tar Pits, and the White Sands Missile Range. But there is another key feature—unlike the other ads in this section, Nike's rely also on detailed copy to set a stage, on which the shoes are wittily associated with the beginning of life on planet earth.

"MONTY PYTHON'S BACK" AD
CAMPAIGN, 1975
DESIGNER: CHRIS PULLMAN
CLIENT: WGBH BOSTON

WGBH When Chris Pullman was told to promote the return of the hilarious *Monty Python's Flying Circus* to Boston's WGBH in 1975, he was faced with the daunting task of making the advertising of a funny show as funny as the show itself, all without being trite. Though he succeeded in developing an idea that did not mimic the Python humor, he did choose the old "so and so is back" trick. But it works, and the combination of a vintage joke and Monty Python's return attracted viewers in droves.

NEW MUSIC MASK, 1989   ART DIRECTOR/DESIGNER: ALEXANDER ISLEY   CLIENT: BROOKLYN ACADEMY OF MUSIC

PART TWO

What Is Humor?

WHAT IS FUNNY TO ONE IS TRAGEDY TO ANOTHER. INDEED, THE PROCESS AND MEDIA OF MAKING VISUAL HUMOR DIFFER FROM INDIVIDUAL TO INDIVIDUAL. THE FOLLOWING INTERVIEWS WITH DESIGNERS, ART DIRECTORS, AND ILLUSTRATORS ARE EVIDENCE OF THIS: FEW FOLLOW THE SAME PATH, NONE HAS A TESTED FORMULA, AND THE RESPONSES TO QUESTIONS ABOUT WHAT HUMOR IS, WHAT IS FUNNY ABOUT THEIR WORK, AND WHY HUMOR IS IMPORTANT ARE ANSWERED QUITE DIFFERENTLY. SOME SEE HUMOR AS A NATURAL OFFSHOOT OF WHAT THEY DO; OTHERS STRUGGLE FOR FUNNY RESULTS. ALL, HOWEVER, BELIEVE THAT THE ACT OF PLAY, WITH HUMOR AS A RESULT, IS A KEY FACTOR IN MAKING VISUAL COMMUNICATIONS ACCESSIBLE

PAUL RAND: THE PLAY INSTINCT

PAUL RAND IS A GRAPHIC DESIGNER BASED IN CONNECTICUT

WHAT IS THE PLAY INSTINCT? It is the instinct for order, the need for rules that, if broken, spoil the game, create uncertainty and irresolution. "Play is tense," says Johan Huizinga. "It is this element of tension and solution that governs all solitary games of skill . . ." Without play, there would be no Picasso. Without play, there is no experimentation. Experimentation is the quest for answers.

YOU DESIGN AS THOUGH YOU WERE PLAYING A GAME OR PIECING TOGETHER A PUZZLE. WHY DON'T YOU JUST SETTLE ON A FORMULA AND FOLLOW IT THROUGH TO ITS LOGICAL CONCLUSION? There are no formulae in creative work. I do many variations, which is a question of curiosity. I arrive at many different configurations—some just slight variations, others more radical—of an original idea. It is a game of evolution.

THEN THE PLAY INSTINCT IS ENDEMIC TO ALL DESIGN? There can be design without play, but that's design without ideas. You talk to me as if I were a psychologist. I can speak only for myself. Play requires time to make the rules. All rules are custom-made to suit a special kind of game. In an environment in which time is money, one has no time to play. One must grasp at every straw. One is inhibited, and there is little time to create the conditions of play.

IS THERE A DIFFERENCE BETWEEN PLAY AND, SAY, WORK? I use the term *play,* but I mean coping with the problems of form and content, weighing relationships, establishing priorities. Every problem of form and content is different, which dictates that the rules of the game are different too.

IS PLAY HUMOR? OR DO THE TWO HAVE DIFFERENT MEANINGS? Not necessarily. It is one way of working. Its product may be very serious even if its spirit is humorous. I think of Picasso. His famous *Bull's Head,* made up of a bicycle seat and handlebars transformed into the head of a bull, is certainly play and humor. It's curious, a visual pun. Picasso is almost always humorous—but this does not rule out seriousness—when he creates images that are contrary to what one would expect. He might put a fish in a bird cage, or a flower with little bulls climbing up the stem. The notion of taking things out of context and giving them new meanings is inherently funny. My friend [Shigeo] Fukuda, the Japanese designer, is a good candidate for one whose sense of play is pertinent. Almost all of his work is the product of playfulness.

YOU'VE DISCUSSED PLAY AS EXPERIMENTATION. WOULD YOU ALSO DESCRIBE PLAY AS DOING THINGS UNWITTINGLY? I don't think that play is done unwittingly. At any rate, one doesn't dwell over whether it's play or something more serious—one just does it. Why does one want to see something rendered in many different ways? Why does one prefer to see a solution in different color combinations or in different techniques? That is an aspect of the play instinct, although it may also be a kind of satisfaction in being prolific. Still, most of the time, many variations provide a good reason to be confused and indiscriminate. I often have to stand away from a project for a while and return in a few weeks.

AS A PAINTER ONE CAN DO THAT, BUT AS A DESIGNER DO YOU HAVE THE TIME? Sure, I do it. Sometimes I find what's wrong on that second

YALE UNIVERSITY BULLDOG
POSTER, 1989
DESIGNER: PAUL RAND
CLIENT: YALE UNIVERSITY

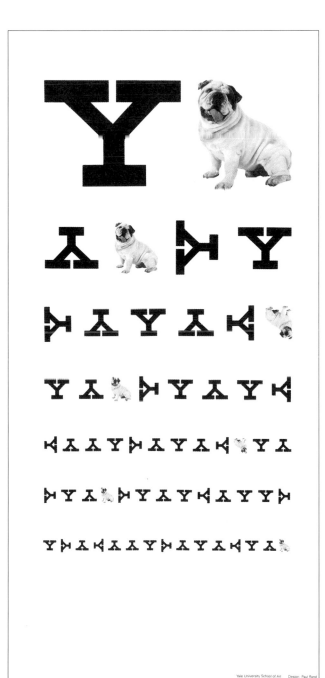

Yale University School of Art   Design: Paul Rand

look. But most of the time the work gets printed, *and then* I see my mistakes. Sometimes I'm able to catch it by having a job reprinted, paying for it myself, or, if the client is generous, by getting him to do it.

A good example of this is the UPS logo [see page 28]. I recently had an interview with a public relations person from UPS about the thirtieth anniversary of the logo. I said that I would like to correct the drawing because some things ought to be changed. I added that I was certain the company would not approve any changes. She tried; regrettably, I was right.

WHAT'S WRONG WITH THE LOGO? IT'S RECOGNIZABLE, AESTHETICALLY PLEASING, AND DISTINCTIVELY WITTY COMPARED TO THE LOGOS OF THE OTHER PACKAGE CARRIERS. Aesthetically pleasing is not aesthetically perfect. There are two problems: One is that the configuration of the bow is unharmonious with the letterform; the other is that the counter of the *p* is incompatible with the other two letters.

BUT THE BOW MAKES IT A PLAYFUL LOGO. Of course it does. In fact, the idea of taking something that's traditionally seen as sacred, the shield, and sort of poking fun at it—which I'm doing by sticking a box on top of it—is a seemingly frivolous gesture. The client, however, never considered it that way, and as it turned out the logo is meaningful because of that lighthearted intent. But that's not the issue. The bow is drawn freely. Today I would use a compass.

ISN'T THE FACT THAT IT IS FREEHAND WHAT GIVES IT THE NEEDED LIGHT TOUCH? Whether a drawing is done with or without the benefit of a tool—the compass—is unimportant. The spirit and intent are what counts. It would be more consistent to construct it geometrically, as are the shield and letters. All elements would be consistent and no one would be the wiser.

For most corporations, their logo is sacrosanct and not meant to be an object of or for humor. Most corporations think the logo is a kind of rabbit's foot or talisman—although sometimes it can be an albatross—and believe that if it is altered, something terrible will happen.

Along those lines, you've designed some of the most recognizable logos in America, specifically the one for IBM. Years later, after you showed how this logo could be applied, you designed a poster that showed the I as an eye, the B as a bee, and the M as itself. You said that the company didn't publish it until some time later. Was that because it poked fun at the company? They thought that it might encourage people working for IBM to misuse or misinterpret the logo. Later, though, they changed their minds, because it didn't become the license they anticipated. What I did turned out to be a humorous idea; in fact, virtually any rebus is a humorous vehicle. Look at the rebuses of Lewis Carroll. A rebus is a form of dramatization making an idea more memorable.

When you begin a project, regardless of medium, are you playing with forms? I don't just play around with form

or forms. That implies a paucity of ideas. I always start with an idea, otherwise I'm working with mere abstractions. It's like taking a trip without a destination. Form develops an idea. You see, form is the manipulation of ideas—or content, if you prefer. And that's exactly what designers are, manipulators of content.

Do you intentionally try to create humorous ideas? No. There are designers with a sense of humor and there are those without. Given the same content, the success is in the delivery. Groucho Marx can make anything funny, while others with similar material might just be tiresome. Still, something can be funny without being humorous—with irony. It helps, of course, if the material is amusing, but someone with a sense of humor can make almost anything funny. How something is done or delivered is often more important than what.

One of your jackets, for a book called Leave Cancelled, comes to mind in this regard. It shows a classical figure flying on a pink background with a number of die-cut bullet holes through the paper. I wouldn't call that funny. The image is Eros, the god of love. That's not inherently funny. The bullet holes have to do with the plot; the protagonist has to return to his regiment before his date is over. Rather than funny, the cover was a literal translation of the plot. For me, a much funnier idea is the H. L. Mencken cover, *Prejudices*. But the solution was

LEAVE CANCELLED BOOK
JACKET, 1945
DESIGNER: PAUL RAND
CLIENT: ALFRED A. KNOPF

PREJUDICES BOOK COVER, 1958
DESIGNER: PAUL RAND
CLIENT: VINTAGE BOOKS

built into the material—I had a lousy photograph of Mencken. What could one do with a bad portrait of the guy? I cut up the photo into a silhouette of someone making a speech, which bore no relation to the shape of the photo. That was funny, in part because of the ironic cropping and because Mencken was such a curmudgeon. But not everything I do is intended to be funny, particularly when the subject matter doesn't warrant it. Conversely, though I try to do things with a certain wit, I don't always succeed.

CAN YOU BE FUNNY WITHOUT A DRAWN LINE? CAN TYPE BE AN ELEMENT OF HUMOR? Of course. One can make letters correspond to an action, like letting them lie down if a text is about resting or dying. Appollinaire did that kind of thing with his concrete poetry. And it was done long before Appollinaire. In Hebrew typography, there's a lot of humor. The way Hebrew was written in the Bible involves all sorts of grammatical tricks. And even when one prays, the prayers are written so that prefixes or suffixes are repeated. These were used as mnemonic devices. Indeed, humor is very Jewish.

JUMPING FROM ANCIENT ISRAEL BACK TO LOGOS, THE NEXT LOGO IS A VERY HUMOROUS APPROACH. Humor was not intended. It's playful and friendly. One critic described it as a child's building block. While that wasn't the idea, it does suggest that association. One can't make people perceive ideas as intended.

Actually, I assumed that Steve Jobs, the founder of NeXT and the man behind the Apple computer, liked cute things, like the Apple logo in rainbow colors with a bite taken out of it. I was told that the reason it was called Apple was that Jobs challenged his staff to come up with an idea—and nobody did—so he decided upon the apple, for no other reason than he liked them. This is a classic example of how arbitrary symbols and logos are—or even should be.

CALLING THE COMPUTER AN APPLE ALSO HUMANIZED IT. Yes, but I think by accident. But it's evidence that a logo does not have to illustrate one's business. If it does, great. Look at the symbol of a bat for Bacardi Rum or the alligator for Lacoste sports clothes. Other than the originator, who really wants a bat or an alligator for their corporate symbol? But these are so ingrained in the consumer's mind that it doesn't really matter. The fact is, if one recognizes the bat or alligator in association with these products, their purpose has been served. The function of a signature, which is what a logo really is, is to be authoritative and not necessarily original or humorous.

RIGHT, BUT WE WERE DISCUSSING YOUR REASON FOR SELECTING THE NEXT CUBE. I have a

NeXT Computers logo, 1989
Designer: Paul Rand
Client: NeXT Computers

Yale Accordian, 1990
Designer: Paul Rand
Client: Yale University

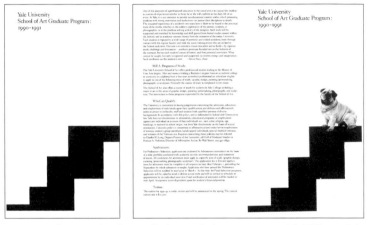

tendency to veer off. The reason was, Jobs liked cutesy things. I believed that I should try to find some kind of object, like a cube. It seemed reasonable, because Jobs indicated that his computer was going to be housed in a cube. He did not say, however, that I should use a cube—he just shot off a bunch of adjectives describing the machine. I thought, what's comparable to a cute little apple? A little cube—something to play with. And it was positioned askew on the envelope, like a Christmas seal.

Someone at the presentation meeting told me that the thing that sold him on this logo was just that—the skewed logos. Which is amusing, because I originally did two versions. The first showed the logo parallel to the picture plane. The only one that was askew was the one on the back of the envelope. While the presentation was being printed, someone asked, "Why don't you do them all like they appear on the envelope?" I agreed. That made it more playful and more lively.

It's like timing in the delivery of a joke. Yes.

Have you ever done parody? I've done a poster for Yale that I would call parody in which I use the step motif—so common today among the trendy. But this old ziggurat motif goes back to ancient times. It is also a common motif in Dutch architecture. It's a common motif that has been dragged out by the Post-Modernists. Because of all this charged meaning, I decided to do a parody of it, just for fun.

It's a recruiting poster in the form of an accordion folder. The cover shows the title and a dramatized rendition of the step motif. When it's opened, the Yale Bulldog is occupying the top step. I'm trying to take the cliché out of clichés. Cezanne's apples were clichés.

Wouldn't you agree with the saying that "nothing is new under the sun?" Everything is a cliché. Almost everything is grist for the creative mill.

Leon Trotsky once wrote that art is a complicated act of twisting and turning old forms that are influenced by stimuli outside of art so that they become new again. I'm not sure what Trotsky means by "old forms." Does he mean old categories, old ideas—the way things used to be done, old content? The designer's problem has always been to do something with content—old or new—to enhance, to intensify, to dramatize, with uncommon ideas or unusual points of view, *and* to see these ideas in a practical way by formal manipulation—sensitive interpretation, with integrity and, if possible, with wit. Mies Van der Rohe once said that being good is more important than being original. Originality is a product, not an intention.

PAULA SCHER: INVOLUNTARY WIT

PAULA SCHER IS A PARTNER IN PENTAGRAM, NEW YORK

OOLA LOGO, 1990
ART DIRECTOR: PAULA SCHER
DESIGNERS: PAULA SCHER,
DEBRA BISHOP
CLIENT: OOLA CORP.

WHY DOES HUMOR ENTER INTO YOUR WORK? I really can't help myself. I think it's because when I was a baby, my mother would tickle me and I giggled, and apparently have never stopped giggling. I think everything has to be funny.

I TAKE THAT TO MEAN YOU ALSO HAVE TO TICKLE OTHERS. SO WHAT MAKES YOUR WORK HUMOROUS? WHAT ABOUT YOUR TYPE OR IMAGE SELECTION CONTRIBUTES TO A HUMOROUS MESSAGE, OR, FOR THAT MATTER, A HUMOROUS STYLE? It's an involuntary process.

YOU MEAN YOU DON'T ENTER INTO A PROJECT WITH THE IDEA OF MAKING A JOKE? No. As a matter of fact, I go into a project with just the opposite thought, because most clients cannot tolerate jokes.

I CAN'T BELIEVE THAT. Most clients don't like funny material. The general comment I hear about my work is that it's too funny. Most clients don't have any sense of humor. And virtually every piece of work I've done has had this problem to some extent, unless I've been totally humorless.

Clients want to be taken seriously, and they want their products to be taken seriously. They want whatever message they are conveying to be taken seriously. So humor is a very hard thing to sell. Most clients don't understand it. They're afraid of it, because in order for something to be funny, it has to be true. And truth is scary.

SO IN YOUR EXPERIENCE, CLIENTS DO NOT YEARN FOR SELF-PARODY? BUT WHAT ABOUT YOUR OOLA CLIENTS? THIS IDENTITY AND PACKAGING PROGRAM FOR AN INTERNATIONAL CHAIN OF CANDY STORES APPEARS TO BE BASED EXCLUSIVELY ON HUMOROUS IDEAS. They're Swedish! They hired me specifically because of my previous work. They looked at my portfolio and based a decision on what they saw, not on extraneous facts like reputation or billing for the past five years. Moreover, they came to me without any preconceived notions. They found my name in the telephone book.

AS I UNDERSTAND YOUR RELATIONSHIP, THEY GAVE YOU CARTE BLANCHE TO DEVELOP AN IDENTITY FROM SCRATCH. IN FACT, THERE WASN'T EVEN A BUSINESS NAME WHEN YOU BEGAN. Right. They were open to my logic and suggestions—and, most importantly, to my humor, because they felt humor would help to create a terrific environment for their store and products.

WHEN THEY CAME TO YOU WITH THIS OPEN-ENDED PROPOSITION, WERE THEY CONSCIOUS THAT THEY WANTED HUMOR? They're selling candy. Candy is fun. They wanted to make candy stores in shopping malls—not an elegant boutique like Godiva or a nonentity like, say, Fanny Farmer. They wanted a strong visual

OOLA BAGS, 1988–1989
ART DIRECTOR: PAULA SCHER
DESIGNERS: PAULA SCHER,
DEBRA BISHOP
CLIENT: OOLA CORP.

statement that would attract customers. So my decision was to make the color palette, stylistic treatment, and even the name seem European. In Europe they are called Sweet Wave, but that is not very imaginative over here, so I decided it should have some Swedish sound. I did two logos—one was a sort of De Stijl design and the other was a face made from letterforms. I presented the two, they liked them both, bought them. The end! After umpteen package designs, not one design for them has been changed.

HOW MANY ITERATIONS OF THE FACE WERE THERE? One. The De Stijl–like logo was purely geometric. My notion was to convey the image of a utopian candy store—I did a few of those. But when I realized that the letters could easily make a face, I used a typeface called Gilles because the Os had eyelashes and the L had a little hook that could be a nose. Actually, the hardest part was deciding on the name. We fooled around for two weeks with various names. The logo itself took only about a minute to design.

LET'S TALK ABOUT THE ALBUM COVER FOR LAKE. IS THIS WHAT WE'D CALL A VISUAL PUN? Yes, the image is a pun. But the story behind this album is especially interesting because it involves the problem that comes into play with humorous illustration: People just don't take it for what it's worth.

Lake is a German band. They might have selected the name because they're from northern Germany, near a lot of lakes. But they had released seven albums and wanted to have an identity that would continue as a series. So I decided that the solution was to create situations that were puns on the word *lake*. My first idea was to show an overflowing sink, which somehow implies a lake—well, at least a flood. I hired Jim McMullan to do the paintings because he worked in watercolors, so that would add another dimension to it.

THAT McMULLAN'S A WATERCOLORIST IS A KIND OF SECONDARY JOKE, ISN'T IT? Perhaps. But more important, his work has a very fluid quality. It's not as hard-edged as an oil or acrylic painting. It's not as whimsical as a cartoon rendering, either. But Jim is very serious about his projects and invests a lot of energy in his work. While he appreciated that this idea was a pun, he also felt that the idea was rather flat. He felt that an overflowing sink is not as interesting as an overflowing sink with somebody in the picture watching it happen. It makes the idea a little more ominous and a bit

LAKE ALBUM JACKETS
ART DIRECTOR/DESIGNER: PAULA SCHER
ILLUSTRATOR: JAMES MCMULLAN
CLIENT: CBS RECORDS

WE THREE KINGS ALBUM JACKET, 1990
DESIGNER: PAULA SCHER
ILLUSTRATOR: BRAD HOLLAND
CLIENT: PARADOX RECORDS, MCA

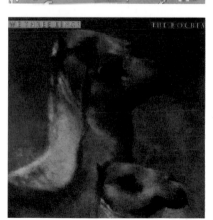

more funny. If a sink overflows and no one's there, who cares? So he painted a pussycat sitting on the sink top, watching the flood in process. That's were the trouble began.

The company had accepted the notion of a painting of a flood alone. The pussycat threw them. They insisted it had to go because "pussycats are not rock and roll animals." I asked what "rock and roll animals" were, and they said, "lions and tigers." I pointed out that lions and tigers were also cats, but the company wasn't impressed. The cover was ultimately saved because a powerful new manager, who liked pussycats, intervened.

But this is the quintessential problem with any kind of humor cover. Clients invariably scrutinize the elements and miss the point. There is a happy ending, though: The next cover had a goat on it, and nobody even questioned whether it was a rock and roll beast.

SPEAKING OF ANIMALS, YOU DESIGNED AN ALBUM FOR THE ROCHES THAT SHOWS THREE CAMELS PAINTED BY BRAD HOLLAND. I NEVER KNEW THAT CAMELS COULD ROCK AND ROLL EITHER. WAS THE ALBUM ABOUT DESERTS OR SAND? No. It was a Christmas album called *We Three Kings*. And frankly, there is no worse cliché than a Christmas album. I knew that the cover would be witless if I put the Three Kings on—since everybody expects it, there's no surprise. Showing camels is amusing yet logical because we all know that the kings rode camels. This is what brings wit into the work.

BUT CAMELS THEMSELVES ARE NOT INHERENTLY FUNNY. DOESN'T WIT COME WITH THE RENDERING? THEY COULD BE CARTOONS OR QUITE REALISTIC—WHY DID YOU DECIDE ON THE LATTER? It was marketed to be a Christmas record with mass appeal, so to make them funny cartoon animals would be wrong. I decided to hire an artist who would paint impressionistic camels—a way of integrating wit with beauty. And the result was wonderful.

SO WHAT WAS THE REACTION THIS TIME? The record label people said, "We don't want no dirty, stinkin', rotten camels on our record cover." However, once again the band overruled the company, with only one silly caveat: I had to put a star on the back cover to make certain that everyone would know it was a Christmas album.

AIGA ANNUAL BOOK JACKET, 1990
DESIGNER/ILLUSTRATOR: PAULA SCHER
CLIENT: AMERICAN INSTITUTE
OF GRAPHIC ARTS

LET'S TALK ABOUT THE COVER FOR THE [1990] AIGA ANNUAL. IS THIS ALSO A VISUAL PUN? No. It's simply obsessive, irrelevant, and useless information intended to satirically represent the process of design. You see, designers are constantly charged with the task of ordering typographic information and conveying clear messages. Here is a message that is not conveyed clearly because the entire composition is sloppy. The joke, however, is that the information is useless and untrue. There's a map of the United States on the back that has states in the wrong place, because I did it from memory and forgot some. On the front cover, I've got a listing of every state in the United States with made-up percentages of the number of people in each state that use Helvetica. Now, who needs to know that? And if they did, they're certainly not learning it here. Then there's a system of absurd color chips on the bottom with colors like *I-U-D* and *A-OK*. Finally, there's a litany of designer's thoughts put in a circle around the eye, such as babble about whether less is more or more is less.

WAS THE PROCESS OF COMING UP WITH THESE GAGS IMMEDIATE? OR DID YOU TRY OUT MANY IDEAS TO GET TO ONE? I approached it like any design job, but as I became more and more obsessive about it, it gained a life of its own. I deliberately made a busy cover because many designers believe that design should be clean and anal—*less is more*. So then I raised the question about whether or not less is really more. As you read the stuff inside the eyeball, it gets sillier: "Less is more, unless less is less, which means that more is more, furthermore, less more may be more than more more, or more less is less than less less, unless, less more and more less are equal—more or less."

DID YOU HAVE ANY PROBLEM GETTING THIS APPROVED? The timing was right, and the cover was accepted without a hitch. The publisher was feeling that the AIGA annual covers were getting a little too stiff, and wanted something "less corporate."

IS HUMOR IN DESIGN ESSENTIALLY A PROCESS OF GETTING AWAY WITH SOMETHING? Always, though it shouldn't be. I find an enormous amount of my work comes out of rebellion. When clients want to present themselves seriously, then I want to take all the seriousness out. Conversely, every time I have worked on a job that is intentionally humorous, like parody books, I am not funny. There's no fun in it. If the whole point of the assignment is to be funny, then what's the joke?

ALEX ISLEY: IN ON THE IN-JOKE

ALEX ISLEY IS THE PRINCIPAL OF ALEX ISLEY DESIGN IN NEW YORK CITY

ISLEY ARCHITECTS "PLACE & TRACE"
TEMPLATE, 1986
ART DIRECTOR/DESIGNER: ALEXANDER ISLEY
CLIENT: ISLEY ARCHITECTS, INC.,
DURHAM, N.C.

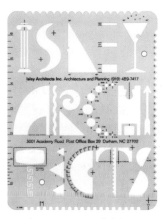

HOW DOES HUMOR ENTER INTO YOUR WORK? The more interesting we can make our work, the more effectively it can reach people. Humorous things are generally pretty interesting to look at, whether they are book jackets that make me smile or the fat man in the checkered suit that I saw this morning chasing a cab. In either case, I know I spend more time thinking about humorous things.

Saying this, I come across as calculating—as if by the precise and subtle use of humor I can inflict more cleverly effective graphic design upon an unsuspecting public. But I'm not that shrewd. Actually, I design things that I think are funny because it makes my job more interesting. That said, a lot of my design is not humorous. In fact, I don't want to be pegged as someone who can only design goofy things.

SOME GRAPHIC HUMOR IS STRAINED. I DON'T SENSE THAT IN YOUR WORK. Sometimes humor makes my work seem less labored. Sometimes a design can get so overwrought that adding a little bit of levity helps get the idea across. I don't know any better way to make contact with an audience. The real challenge for me is making my work appear natural and effortless.

YOU STILL HAVE TO CONVINCE A CLIENT THAT THE HUMOROUS SOLUTION IS BEST. True. But I don't try to ram it down their throats either. Some problems are obviously not appropriate for a humorous solution. Conversely, some clients who take themselves too seriously need to be told to lighten up.

THROUGH WHAT MEANS DO YOU ACHIEVE HUMOROUS DESIGN? Sometimes it comes across in the text, other times as visual jokes. A few years ago, I did a promotion piece for my father, an architect. He wanted a simple brochure, but I wanted something a little less conventional and more useful. So I designed an architectural template that spelled out the name of his firm using architectural shapes. Since it was a tangible product, recipients were hard pressed to throw it away. It also took a mild poke at his firm, because I used the shapes of toilets, bathtubs, and so on to spell out his name.

To accept a design like this takes a certain level of self-assurance, which is rare to find in a client, especially when the financial stakes are high. Overall, I've been pretty good at selling my ideas to clients who are not my relatives.

WITH THE TEMPLATE, YOU FOUND THE ELEMENTS OF HUMOR WITHIN THE PROBLEM ITSELF. THE TEMPLATE IS A COMMON DESIGN TOOL. SO YOU TWISTED THE LOGICAL INTO THE ABSURD. That's the root of humor. It rarely works to use a joke or visual pun arbitrarily. The goal must always be to make a connection with audiences by using something close to their own experience, not just impose a style or idea on people because it's your nature.

DECIDING WHAT CAN OR CANNOT BE TWISTED IS AN INTUITIVE THING, TOO. SOME CLIENTS CAN GO EITHER WAY. FOR EXAMPLE, I'VE SEEN VERY SIMPLE, STRAIGHTFORWARD PROMOTIONAL MATERIAL FOR THE BROOKLYN ACADEMY OF MUSIC BY OTHER DESIGNERS. BUT YOUR WORK FOR THE SAME CLIENT IS SILLY IN THE BEST SENSE. You are speaking about a promotion for the New Music America Festival. They said we could do whatever we wanted, but, oddly, we were prevented from using images symbolizing "new music" or "America." The problem was to make the notion of "new music" appealing to a wide audience. There's a popular conception that "new music" means that it was made by chainsaws or other oddball instruments—and in some cases, it's true. But to dispel that notion, we decided to use a stock photograph of a goofy, smiling boy as our mascot.

New Music America isn't inherently humorous. In fact, BAM considers it pretty serious. But we wanted a poster that would make the viewer curious. And there were two positive effects with our laughing kid: One is that when people see that kind of photograph, they smile or laugh to themselves, because it's not threatening. But it was sort of mysterious. And the type and the image had little in common. Yet it served to pull in passersby.

HOW MANY IDEAS DID YOU TRY BEFORE DECIDING ON THE FACE? AFTER ALL, IT COULD HAVE BEEN ANY FACE, RIGHT? We offered three ideas to the client. Despite their restrictions, we did do a very literal version. Another was a big die-cut sticker saying "New," printed in fluorescent ink about three feet across. We planned to plaster it around town atop other existing posters. It was a commentary, of sorts, on the way posters in the street obliterate each other. The last was the smiling kid. We looked at about 40 pictures before selecting the one we liked, and the reason for choosing him had to do with the goofy factor. Though I like to rationally explain my decisions, sometimes it comes down to instinct.

I GUESS THAT NOSTALGIC LEAVE IT TO BEAVER QUALITY GIVES IT MORE POWER AS A HUMOROUS DEVICE. WHERE DID IT COME FROM? From an old stock-photography catalog. The kid's probably around 45 years old now, and if he saw it he'd probably be shocked to see himself so immortalized. We made certain, however, that it was fully photo-released.

HOW MUCH OF YOUR HUMOR RELIES ON THE AUDIENCE HAVING PREVIOUS KNOWLEDGE OF EXISTING REFERENCES? Though I hope that not much of it is an in-joke, most of my design humor depends on knowing the language of signs and symbols. Shared reference *is* a requirement. This is important for all effective communication. If people don't recognize the references, then the joke fails, and so does the designer.

LHS&B dairy promotion, 1990
Art Director: Alexander Isley
Designer: Carrie Leeb
Client: Levine Huntley Schmidt
and Beaver, Inc., and Christopher
Vincent, Inc.

SPY magazine—various issues,
1987–1988
Art Director: Alexander Isley
Designers: Catherine Gilmore-
Barnes, Alexander Knowlton
Client: Spy Publishing Partners

ISN'T MOST DESIGN HUMOR A KIND OF IN-JOKE? It has had to rely on shared references. If a poster or brochure has to appeal to a wider audience, you can't be too specific. For New Music America, the goofy kid probably would appeal to more people than if we made a joke about electronic keyboards.

DO YOU USE CLICHÉS OR STEREOTYPES? There is always a need to reinterpret clichés rather than just copy them. Almost all design is based on clichés—symbols and words that our culture readily understands. But I'd be disappointed if we could only use clichés to make effective humor. Designers rely on things like strange typefaces or putting photographs at weird rakish angles to somehow signal the fact that something

fact that this agency prides itself on unconventional approaches, it was a tough sell to get them to do something as overtly bizarre as this. But coming up with something funny was also tough, because everything had to be scrutinized by their new business department—the death knell always sounds any time a project requires committee approval. Fortunately, they went ahead with it, and I understand it was very successful.

YOU ARE KNOWN FOR UNCONVENTIONAL APPROACHES. WHY WOULD A CLIENT COME TO YOU OTHERWISE? A lot of my success with humor or being irreverent is because I am small potatoes. I mostly have small clients, and with them I can get away with a lot more. I told one

funny is going on. I try to stay away from that. It's easy to wear a clown suit before you tell the joke; it's much funnier, however, if you tell a joke when your wearing a tuxedo.

WHAT WAS YOUR MOST DIFFICULT PIECE TO MAKE WORK HUMOROUSLY? To help an advertising agency get dairy accounts, we did a promotion where we had some guy in Vermont make weathervanes with a cow as the centerpiece. Instead of North, East, South and West, we used the agency's initials—*L, H, S,* and *B*. Despite the

client that in each issue of his newsletter, I will do one thing that will make him nervous. If I don't, then he will know I'm getting lazy.

WHAT WAS YOUR MOST SUCCESSFUL HUMOROUS PIECE? I did a catalog, again for the Brooklyn Academy of Music—I guess they're turning into my best client for such things. It was for a fund-raising auction at which they sold off everything from tickets to the Rolling Stones in London to a commitment that Andrée Putman will design your bathroom. It was pretty high-

BAM AUCTION BIDDING KIT, 1990
ART DIRECTOR: ALEXANDER ISLEY
DESIGNER/ILLUSTRATOR:
LYNETTE CORTEZ
COPYWRITER: ALEXANDER ISLEY
CLIENT: BROOKLYN ACADEMY OF MUSIC

SPY KIT, 1987
ART DIRECTOR/DESIGNER/COPYWRITER:
ALEXANDER ISLEY
CLIENT: SPY MAGAZINE

ticket stuff for which they needed a catalog. The problem was that, due to the late submissions of the items, the catalog could not be printed until the last minute. Obviously, that made it impossible to design and print something elaborate, so we developed a clipboard for them with a wraparound four-color cover that could be printed in advance. Each person got an auction kit, which included a pen—the BAM-O-Matic Bidmaster 2000—and an auction paddle designed as a hand on a stick.

Using the clipboard as our outer cover, everything else could be designed on the Mac-

intosh the day before and sent directly to a quickie printer who did it in a day. So BAM bypassed having to print an expensive book, but the result was engaging. That night, the people were having a good time with it, which put them in a lighthearted mood. And being a little giddy makes it easier to throw more money around.

THIS EVENT WASN'T INHERENTLY HUMOROUS. SO BY DESIGNING SOMETHING FUNNY, YOU IMPOSED ANOTHER LEVEL OF BEHAVIOR ON THE CROWD. IT COMES DOWN TO THE POWER OF SURPRISE. HOWEVER, WHEN YOU ARE DESIGNING SOMETHING PURPOSEFULLY HUMOROUS,

LIKE SPY MAGAZINE, ISN'T IT HARDER TO BE FUNNY? It can, but it's difficult to speak about *Spy* in that context. Sure, it would be hard to design a comedy magazine, but *Spy* is not a comedy magazine. Unlike the *National Lampoon*, *Spy* has always tried to portray itself as being truthful. In the beginning, the premise was that all the stories would be based on fact—good writing and solid reporting. So stories would be designed with a documentary feel rather than forced into esoteric, goofy layouts.

NEVERTHELESS, SPY USES GRAPHIC CONVENTIONS THAT SUGGEST A COMEDIC SPIRIT. People say that the various color tints, small silhouetted photographs, and various conflicting typefaces made it look wacky, but the fact is, we only used three typefaces, few tints, the photos were appropriate, and things weren't bouncing all over. But the design only supported the written humor.

BUT YOU'VE CREATED A NEW CUE FOR HUMOR. YOU MIGHT NOT PUT PHOTOS ON STUPID ANGLES, BUT YOU USE TINY SILHOUETTED PICTURES THAT MOST TIMES MAKE THE SUBJECTS LOOK LUDICROUS. And that was stolen from old *Modern Screen* magazines. Indeed, there was a visual equivalent to what the editors were saying in words. There were also a lot of little inside jokes that the careful reader would begin to recognize over time. But that's the beauty about working for a magazine where presumably you have a captive audience. After a month, you can do variations on a theme that you've previously established. It's quite different from doing a poster or other one-shot piece. In a magazine, the humor can build over time; in a poster, the jokes must be more immediate.

MIKE HICKS IS PRESIDENT OF HIXO, INC, IN DALLAS

DO YOU HAVE A PHILOSOPHICAL REASON FOR USING HUMOR IN YOUR WORK? It's cheap. Let's face it, if I had all the money in the world, I guess I would probably have loftier ideas. But my clients, especially my clients in Texas, are not what I would call flush at the moment. I suppose that's as good a reason as any for using humor. But there's another: Humor sells.

YOU MEAN HUMOR IS A WAY OF FORGING SOME KIND OF RELATIONSHIP BETWEEN CLIENT AND CONSUMER? It's probably the most effective way. Well, humor and anger, that is. If you are angry and it comes through, like in political posters, the common bond is hatred—which is a field that I hope to get into real soon.

HOW DOES HUMOR MANIFEST ITSELF IN YOUR WORK? It's usually stamped out early on.

STAMPED OUT BY WHOM? By clients! Humor puts clients in a very unusual position, because they have to choose between the effectiveness of humor and the possibility of alienating the audience. The downside is that humor is relative—I might do something that I think is terribly funny, and someone else will hate it.

A great example of that is, some years back, Hixo did a controversial Christmas card. I thought it would be a hoot to have Rudolph the Red-Nosed Reindeer being cooked on a spit. And we did a little silhouette drawing—not grisly or anything—of him over an open fire. Everyone in the office thought it was funny, so we blithely mailed it all over. As you might imagine, however, some were returned to us with

scathing notes about how I'd ruined Christmas.

YOU INSENSITIVE BRUTE, FOR SOME PEOPLE IT'S LIKE BURNING THE AMERICAN FLAG. For some people that's exactly right. Anyway, several years later I was judging *Communication Arts*'s annual show and there was a drawing of a reindeer salami. Someone had taken a salami and done a high-design packaging job. It was funny and very well designed. Because it was a borderline thing, I urged the other judges to include it in the show. One judge just hated it, saying it was too offensive. He also said that it reminded him of "this jerk," who, a couple of years earlier, sent out a Christmas card with a reindeer on a spit. "It just ruined Christmas for me and my children," he said and continued this long diatribe about how life in New York was tough enough. Christmas was the one time of the year when you really got into traditions, and he didn't want anybody screwing with them. Of course, the jerk was me! I still have a big supply of these cards and continue to send them out every year.

THAT'S THE POWER OF A DRAWN OR NARRATIVE IMAGE. IS THERE SUCH A THING AS PURE DESIGN HUMOR? Maybe real complex humor is tough to do with design. But I think there are certainly words that sometimes can mean one thing yet, by the way in which they are designed, can mean another. For the 1988 AIGA National Conference, I did a brochure on the theme of "Dangerous Ideas." It was full of little visual puns, like a sign that said "Slippery When Wet," showing a car sliding off the sign, or

"DANGEROUS IDEAS AHEAD"
BROCHURE, 1989
ART DIRECTOR/DESIGNER: MIKE HICKS
ILLUSTRATION: HARRISON SAUNDERS
CLIENT: AMERICAN INSTITUTE OF
GRAPHIC ARTS

CHUY'S NEW AGE TEX-MEX
LOGOETTE, 1990
DESIGNER: MIKE HICKS
CLIENT: COMIDA DELUXE

"NEW TRICKS FROM AN OLD FRIEND"
ADS, 1990
ART DIRECTOR: DUANA GILL
DESIGNER: MIKE HICKS
CLIENT: RYAN MCFARLAND CO.

a "One Way" sign with arrows in two directions. There are always ways in which you can make something funny by creating a tension between what a thing is saying and what it actually is. I don't know if those are real knee-slappers, but cumulatively in one piece, they can project and attitude that pure design—design without humor—often cannot do.

GENERALLY, ARE YOU STARTING WITH THE VERBAL HUMOR AND DESIGNING AN APPROPRIATE MOTIF? OR DO YOU START WITH A VISUAL IDEA AND THEN WRITE THE TEXT? It depends on the use. There are lots of people who can write funny material. Indeed, the easy way is to come up with something funny and then illustrate it; the hardest is to create comedy without words.

GIVE ME AN EXAMPLE. We did what I call logoettes for a Mexican restaurant named Chuy's. The images are not Mexican motifs, but rather little spaceships and globes. The restaurant is new age Tex-Mex. One image shows an infant's face with rings and moons, like Saturn, around its head. The image is inherently funny because of a kind of kitsch sensibility. It's akin to a cult in Texas that built itself around a guy named Bob. He's an imaginary character, a sort of Ward Cleaver guy, whose image comes from those 1950s clip-art books.

WHAT MAKES THE BOB CHARACTER SO FUNNY? IS IT JUST THAT HE'S TAKEN OUT OF CONTEXT IN THE 1990S? I'M CERTAIN THAT THAT "TYPICAL" AMERICAN MALE IMAGE WAS TAKEN QUITE SERIOUSLY IN THE 1950S. Using art like that is like trying to travel cross-country today in a 1950s Oldsmobile station wagon. The culture has progressed at such lightning speed and has left so many anachronisms behind—it's not just one generation removed, it's like 20 generations removed. Things old-fashioned are funny. How we perceived ourselves can also be funny, mostly because of the naiveté of the images.

WE LAUGH AT THE PAST, BUT STILL YOU EMBRACE ITS ARTIFACTS. Because it's comfortable, distressingly so, in the context of modern life.

IS YOUR APPROACH BASED ON RECAPTURING THE PAST, AND THEREBY GIVE COMFORT TO YOUR AUDIENCE? Not necessarily. I don't think that nostalgia is our funniest stuff. In fact, the funniest is often slightly uncomfortable for the living—it's too easy to make fun of the dead. Now we've used our share of matchbook clips, but really the tough part of being funny is to be relevant. I hope that every so often we are.

ETIENNE DELESSERT: ALLEGORICAL HUMOR

ETIENNE DELESSERT IS AN ILLUSTRATOR AND ANIMATOR
BASED IN LAKEVILLE, CONNECTICUT

ASHES ASHES IS TOLD THROUGH HUMOROUS CHARACTERS, BUT YOUR MESSAGE IS QUITE SERIOUS. THIS IS A TIME-HONORED CONVENTION AMONG CARTOONISTS AND SATIRISTS. IS SERIOUSNESS CUT WITH WIT THE BEST WAY TO TELL A MORAL TALE TO CHILDREN OR TO ADULTS? Children get a lot of bad information these days from TV and the media. Not just information about man-made problems, but natural disasters, too. The idea that a city can be wiped out by an earthquake is chilling even for an adult—more frightening than the threat of war. Kids know more about this now than when I was a child because of the daily bombardment of news. Having this fear, which I'm certain I share with others, I wonder if it is still worth working, loving, or having kids. And I find that there are two ways to react: One is to succumb, the other is to talk about the common experience. In my case, the latter happens to be through telling stories in books.

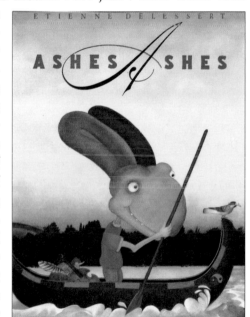

HOW IS HUMOR A VEHICLE FOR THAT KIND OF COMMUNICATION? Surprise is a way of disorienting the enemy. It's like walking around a large rock, and so changing it's shape, discovering new cracks and folds, defining new lights and deep shadows.

LET'S TALK SPECIFICALLY ABOUT ASHES ASHES. DOES THE TITLE REFER TO THE BIBLICAL REFERENCE, "ASHES TO ASHES, DUST TO DUST?" No, it comes from the nursery rhyme "Ring around the Rosy." You know, "Ashes, ashes, we all fall down." Indeed, I interpret it as after going through all of life's activities, we die, things disappear, yet other things continue. The myth of the Phoenix.

HOW DOES THIS APPLY TO YOUR STORY? The main character, who by the way is neither child nor adult, is coming home from a trip to nowhere. The reader assumes that he's returning to a normal, peaceful life. But it develops that three strangers have been waiting for him for a long, long time. After he returns they knock on the door. But they don't say who they are—

ARE THEY THE THREE WISE MEN? Well, they are like itinerant sages who went from village to village centuries ago, offering their prophecies about the world, trying to change people to believe in some righteous force. Some believed them, others ran them out of town.

THEY ARE LIKE THE CARTOON CLICHÉ OF THE DOOMSAYER WEARING SACKCLOTH AND ASHES. READING ABOUT THEM IN YOUR TEXT, I SENSE THE DEVIL IS AT PLAY. WAS YOUR INTENT TO MAKE THEM COMEDIC? Giving them faces was the most difficult casting problem in the book. I had trouble reconciling how I described them in words to what they became in the picture. One

JACKET (ON PAGE 137) AND INTERIOR
PAGES FROM <u>ASHES ASHES</u>, 1990
DESIGNER: RITA MARSHALL
ILLUSTRATOR/WRITER:
ETIENNE DELESSERT
CLIENT: STEWART TABORI AND CHANG

man is sterner than the other two, who are more comedic. I made them so because I know that if some ominous strangers came to my door, I might not open up. So they had to be somewhat charming.

BUT THESE STRANGERS ARE TELLING YOUR CHARACTER TO DO SOMETHING ABSURD: TO CHANGE HIS PHYSICAL APPEARANCE FROM HUMAN TO SOMETHING THAT'S AT ONCE MONSTROUS AND LUDICROUS, IN ORDER THAT HE MIGHT FIND TRUTH SOMEWHERE. Actually, they don't give him any choice. Like witches or magicians, they change him and tell him that he'll only return to his human form after he finds the truth, sending him on a journey so vague that he will have to rediscover himself.

WHY WAS HE SELECTED? Fate. They approached anyone they could. He didn't protest. I think he was just fed up with things as they were. He wanted a change of identity and life.

IS THIS AUTOBIOGRAPHICAL? YOU GAVE UP A STUDIO WITH MANY EMPLOYEES AND A LIFE IN SWITZERLAND TO MOVE TO THE NORTHERNMOST PART OF CONNECTICUT TO WORK ESSENTIALLY ALONE WITH YOUR WIFE. Though it can be interpreted that way, it's never stated clearly that I am the little guy. Sure, I was able to have this idea because I've had a similar experience, but there are lots of people who want to be left alone these days. And this allows a broad basis to the story.

WHY DID YOU DESIGN A CHARACTER THAT LOOKS PART RABBIT AND PART CROCODILE? It had to be a composite. I didn't want it to be just a mouse, for instance, or a rabbit or squirrel, because each has a specific human connotation.

So in this case, the body is almost like that of a boy, and his form suggests basic human personality traits. But he is also part rabbit, because the rabbit has forever been a character of fantasy and dream. Everything is sign, and sign becomes a symbol.

IT IS A BITTERSWEET STORY, WITH A BITTERSWEET CHARACTER. Correct. All of a sudden, he can become quite angry. You can see he has teeth, and so can be biting. But he also has fluffy ears to offset the monstrous parts. I wanted him to be an enigma.

HE ALSO LOOKS LIKE A GARGOYLE. AND REFERRING BACK TO YOUR STATEMENT ABOUT USING HISTORY, THE GARGOYLE IS THE ROOT OF CARICATURE. Gargoyles are sublime in the sense that they are composite monsters. Back in the Middle Ages, there was some humor in showing ghosts and monsters on the house of God. It was also a way of professing an ambiguous attitude toward God and religion.

WHY DO YOU HAVE THIS CHARACTER MEET OTHERS WHO LOOK EXACTLY LIKE HIMSELF? RATHER THAN MONSTERS, TOGETHER THEY LOOK LIKE A TRIBE OF LITTLE ELVES. If he was alone, the story would be much more scary. Just the idea of multiplying the character in a family of lookalikes allowed me to describe the ambiguity of the "redemption" and to emphasize the fragility of the group, as well as to encourage the main character to look within himself for answers.

ANOTHER ABSURDITY IN <u>ASHES ASHES</u> IS THE IDEA THAT THIS TRIBE OF LOVELY MONSTERS CAN ACTUALLY BUILD A PERFECT SHAKER

HOUSE. GIVEN THEIR APPEARANCE, ONE ASSUMES THAT THEY CANNOT FUNCTION EFFECTIVELY IN SOCIETY. WHAT DOES THIS REAL-WORLD CONSTRUCTION BY UNREAL CHARACTERS SYMBOLIZE? I live in a mythical world, where stones can talk and birds sing with the shrieking voices of my ancestors. So it is perfectly normal for my characters, representing people I have known, to behave as if they were in the "real" world.

IS THIS A PARABLE ABOUT LIFE'S CHANGES NOT BEING ALL THAT THEY'RE CRACKED UP TO BE? OR ARE YOU MAKING THE STATEMENT THAT IN TIME, PEOPLE WILL INVARIABLY BECOME BORED WITH WHATEVER THEY'RE DOING? It's sad, but true, and I have experienced it. When an activity is satisfying for many years, it makes me wonder if I should not be doing something else? I like surprise in my life. By surprise I mean that initial moment when you think about a brand-new concept and attempt to make it work.

HOW DOES <u>ASHES ASHES</u> PURGE YOU OF YOUR DEMONS? There was no purge. I have added a few more monsters to my circus. I am waiting for the right moment to climb on seven clouds and fly away.

SINCE WE'VE ESTABLISHED THAT THERE IS AN AUTOBIOGRAPHICAL COMPONENT TO <u>ASHES ASHES</u>, WITH MANY LEVELS OF MEANING, IS THE PICTORIAL AND VERBAL LANGUAGE THAT YOU'VE CHOSEN APPROPRIATE FOR YOUR AUDIENCE? Is this book for children or adults, or both? In the way that books are basically read by adults to children, I hope that the adult will understand enough of the story to share it with the child, and that the child will enjoy the pictures because they are different from his everyday experience. And this last point is why I require humor. For I take chunks of the real world and turn them on the side.

IN OTHER WORDS, YOU'RE USING HUMOR TO GRAPPLE WITH AN OTHERWISE EMOTIONALLY DIFFICULT SUBJECT, AND ALSO TO GIVE YOUR YOUTHFUL READERS SOMETHING TO CHALLENGE THEIR IMAGINATION. IF YOU WERE TO TELL THIS STORY WITHOUT METAPHOR, IT WOULD NO LONGER BE A STORY, BUT A CONFESSION. Humor is helping to build a story. Of course, it can take a trauma and translate it into unthreatening terms, because it is a means of separating the naked you from the symbolic you. When I think about my humor, it can be angry, but it's not black. And in this way, I hope my stories will live in people's minds for many years—from child- to adulthood. I feel I am building something with my books, one brick at a time, to slow the erosion, so children can find a garden to play, a land "where even dust would taste sweet, like white flour on warm oatmeal bread."

STEPHEN DOYLE: AIN'T MISBEHAVIN'

STEPHEN DOYLE IS A PARTNER IN DRENTTEL DOYLE PARTNERS, NEW YORK CITY

BELOW: HB MAGAZINE, 1989
CREATIVE DIRECTOR, ART DIRECTOR, DESIGNERS: STEPHEN DOYLE, TOM KLUEPFEL
CLIENT: CREATIVE REVIEW MAGAZINE, LONDON

BOTTOM RIGHT: CAROLINE'S COMEDY CLUB ADVERTISEMENT, 1988
CREATIVE DIRECTOR: STEPHEN DOYLE
ART DIRECTOR/DESIGNER: ROSEMARIE TURK
PHOTOGRAPHER: GEORGE HEIN
CLIENT: CAROLINE'S COMEDY CLUB

MAKING THE BIBLE INTO A MONTHLY MAGAZINE IS AN INSPIRED SATIRE. INDEED, GIVEN THE WAY RELIGION IS PACKAGED THESE DAYS, THE IDEA IS NOT EVEN LUDICROUS. HOW DID IT COME ABOUT? *HB* [*Holy Bible*] was initiated by a British magazine who asked 12 design firms and advertising agencies to repackage the Bible. Most people approached it as a standard graphic problem, resulting in beautiful book designs. We, however, thought that a magazine would be a really versatile and lively format for the Bible, because there's so much spin-off material about life-style, cooking, entertaining, and stuff like that.

Since nobody can read the Bible in one sitting, and people don't like to read anymore anyway, our proposal was to turn it into a monthly. YOU BRILLIANTLY ADAPTED THE FORMAT OF HG, THE HOME AND LIFE-STYLE MAGAZINE. *House and Garden* had recently changed to *HG* and I had been hired to redesign one of its incarnations. Once we decided that the Bible *was* a magazine, we had to come up with a perfect model. *HG* made perfect sense.

HOW LONG DID THE PROCESS OF CREATION TAKE? SEVEN DAYS? Two weeks to get it off the ground. And then some further time to design it and photograph the comps on a red satin background with some of God's light pouring in.

DOES A SENSE OF HUMOR FREQUENTLY APPEAR IN YOUR WORK? Ours is not really ever ha-ha funny. We try to do engaging rather than knee slapping work. We believe that if you can make people smile, you've got 'em. There's a lot of distrust of printed things these days. For decades, ads have been telling us that Product X is the best, and people have really learned to distrust that kind of hyperbole.

Indeed, the increase in distrust corresponds to a new ethos for the '90s—stay-home-have-a-family values have replaced make-a-lot-of-money values. Things communicate best on a personal level. And one way to get personal fast without getting into therapy is to make messages at least slightly humorous.

LET'S TALK ABOUT ANOTHER WITTY STRATEGY: THE SUBWAY AND TRAIN STATION POSTERS FOR OLYMPIA & YORK, ANNOUNCING THE OPENING OF THE WORLD FINANCIAL CENTER IN MANHATTAN. Nobody really knew where Olympia & York's World Financial Center was, despite the fact its the largest real estate development in North America. Our job was to put it on the map. We had to deal both with a critical lack of awareness and a small budget with which to do it. The World Financial Center sounds like the last place on earth anybody would want to go to. So a big part of our job was to subvert the seriousness of

WORLD FINANCIAL CENTER AD CAMPAIGN, 1988
CREATIVE DIRECTOR: TOM KLUEPFEL
ART DIRECTOR/DESIGNER: ANDREW GRAY
PHOTOGRAPHER: PETER AARON
CLIENT: OLYMPIA & YORK

the name and make it seem like a place that's worth a visit. Our strategy was to make a game.

We developed a series of teaser posters hung in various locations found by drawing concentric circles on a map of the tri-state area. We hung them at train stations. The farther away you were from Manhattan, the poster would say, "You're cold, definitely cold." As you got closer, they began to warm up a little, referring to the child's game where you "get warmer" as you get closer to the prize. Also, the closer you got, the larger the buildings on the poster got. And at the bottom of each, there was a payoff line that said something like, "You're definitely cold, but the palm trees downtown are sizzling."

WAS ARRIVING AT THIS IDEA A DIFFICULT PROCESS? IT SEEMS LIKE IT'S ONE OF THOSE IDEAS THAT JUST SEEMS SO EASY, BUT WAS PROBABLY TORTUROUS TO CONCEIVE. The idea hit like lightening. The execution, however, was absolute hell. We made 16 variations of this thing that had to be the right distance from ground zero. And to get them posted in exactly the right places, never overlapping our concentric circles, required great navigational precision on our part. There had to be enough coverage so that an average viewer would see at least two of them to make the idea work.

CAROLINE'S IS A COMEDY NIGHTCLUB. ISN'T IT DIFFICULT TO DO HUMOROUS ADVERTISING FOR

SOMETHING THAT IS ALREADY ABOUT HUMOR? Yes, but in this case, the problem was challenging for another reason: Caroline's is in the funny position of being a comedy club and a restaurant too. So do you say, "come to this comedy club and eat good food"? That doesn't work. Or do you say, "Come to this restaurant and listen to jokes"? That doesn't do it, either. We decided to create a funny image so that people would start talking about the advertising and therefore generate talk about Caroline's itself. What we did was develop a series of posters that lied. When a poster says "Oyster," we show a picture of a shrimp.

DID THIS SUBTERFUGE WORK? Well, it's not great for people who are just learning the English language, but otherwise it did get attention.

SPEAKING OF DESIGNING HUMOROUSLY FOR INHERENTLY HUMOROUS PROJECTS, YOU DEVELOPED THE INITIAL FORMAT FOR SPY MAGAZINE. WAS THAT A PROBLEM OF CREATING NEW SIGNALS AND CODES FOR HUMOR? *Spy* came to us to be their advertising agency when the magazine was just a gleam in their eyes. They had already commissioned someone to design the magazine. It turned out, however, there really wasn't any advertising to do, but the publishers liked our ideas so much they gave us the magazine to design instead of the team that was working on it. Actually, it's a

SPY MAGAZINE, 1986
CREATIVE DIRECTOR/ART DIRECTOR:
STEPHEN DOYLE
DESIGNER: ROSEMARIE TURK
CLIENT: SPY MAGAZINE

DETAIL OF PAGE FROM SPY, 1986
CREATIVE DIRECTOR/ART DIRECTOR:
STEPHEN DOYLE
DESIGNER: ROSEMARIE TURK
CLIENT: SPY MAGAZINE

rather funny situation. They weren't having a design problem per se, but had slammed into a language barrier—the design team was Italian. But *Spy* is rooted in the nuances of the English language. The coeditors, Kurt Andersen and Graydon Carter, are brilliant practitioners of our native tongue—every paragraph is so chock-full of cultural references that it's hard to keep up even if English *is* your native tongue. They've got such a *Leave-It-to-Beaver*-meets-*Wall-Street-Week* vocabulary that a lot was lost in the translation. We were brought in because we understood their vernacular.

DID YOU HAVE A GRAND DESIGN PLAN? BECAUSE IT IS COPIED NOW, SPY IS AN ARCHETYPE OF 1980s MAGAZINE DESIGN. IT'S SO LAYERED WITH INFORMATION, SO FULL OF WHAT I'D CALL VARIOUS DOORS TO OPEN ON THE PAGE, THAT IT REALLY IS A NEW GENRE. We were trying to make a magazine

IS THAT THE REASON FOR THE DIVERSE SIDE-BARS? When I was a designer at *Esquire*, the editors were always saying they had great ideas for side-bars. The entire magazine could have been side-bars if we'd let them. But the designers invariably said the side-bars would ruin their beautiful pages. Conversely, with *Spy*, we decided to give the editors all the side-bars they wanted, including side-bars to side-bars, ad nauseum.

ISN'T THAT EFFECT KIND OF CLOYING? Now it is, because so many others do it. But when we started it, when magazines were so precious and dainty and everyone was trying to spin off hyperclassicism without any real understanding of it, it was a clean breath of "foul air." The difference between *Spy* and its imitators is that *Spy's* design came from the content. I was decorating with information rather than decorating for its own sake.

that would disobey the rules of magazines. So there's lots of type with different leads. There are a lot of different headlines on a page. There's a lot of type that is critically small—almost *too* small. And it's meant to be irritating—or, rather, fun. But the key to the mayhem of *Spy* is accessibility. There wasn't much money for illustration or photography, and we really had to make the type do the talking. So we wanted to make lots of places for the reader to get into the magazine.

MUST EVERYTHING YOU DO EVIDENCE THE WIT OF ITS MAKER? I was the youngest of four boys, all two years apart. As a child, when we gathered around the dinner table, you wouldn't believe all the testosterone at work, as we competed for the attention of two parents. As the smallest, I couldn't compete on their turf, but I soon figured out that if I could be witty—not funny, just witty—I could get the spotlight. Is it surprising that these tactics show up in my work today?

DAVID KAESTLE: DESIGNING HUMOR

COSMOPARODY MAGAZINE PARODY, 1984
ART DIRECTOR/DESIGNER: DAVID KAESTLE
PHOTOGRAPHER: HARRY LANGDON
CLIENT: TSM PUBLISHING CO.

DAVID KAESTLE IS THE PRINCIPAL OF DAVID KAESTLE
DESIGN, NEW YORK CITY

THE DESIGN OF HUMOR INCLUDES MANY FORMS, BUT THE ONE YOU'RE PROBABLY MOST KNOWN FOR IS PARODY. WHAT IS A PARODY? Graphic parody knocks off another form. This can be defined two ways: The first is the specific parody, like a send up of *Playboy* magazine; the second is a genre parody, such as send-ups of cookbooks, fitness guides, and so on. In the first case, the graphic form is totally dictated by the host or target. The look is completely decided. What the designers and writers must do is think of ideas that work within that framework. Good parody is basically *content*-driven, since the *style* is preexisting and, if violated, destroys the illusion.

WOULD IT HARM THE PARODY IF YOU TOOK LIBERTIES OUTSIDE OF THE EXISTING FORM? You take the liberties with content and you leave the "look" intact—that's what makes it funny. The whole magic of doing a good parody is to avoid letting any of your design aesthetic influence the outcome. It is really a perception problem—you must get into your host's head and ask yourself how do the editors and art directors of *Cosmopolitan*, or whatever, *think* about their articles? What makes it *Cosmopolitan*, rather than something else? Anyone can match typefaces and mimic their colors—it's the attitude you have to go after.

Most of the parodies I've done are two-edged, or at least they try to be. I'll illustrate this with the *Spy* magazine parody. It was, in a sense, doing several things at once, unlike some of the more sophomoric parodies like *Doque—Vogue for dogs*—which did not make very good fun of the host publication because it didn't say much about *Vogue*, or even about the high-fashion business. Rather, it was just a set of graphic windows to look at funny pictures of dogs.

SO IT WAS A VEHICLE FOR STUPID ANIMAL JOKES RATHER THAN A COMMENT ON A CULTURAL PHENOMENON? Right. It was not a vicious attack or even a moderately funny critique of the rag trade with all its foibles, stylish inconsistencies, and goofball traditions. It could have been great!

What we tried to do with *Sty* was to not only use the pig as a funny model to put silly clothes on, but to let him be a metaphor for the self-indulgent yuppie reader who we were claiming *Spy* was appealing to. As a subtext, we were also trying to poke fun at all these stupid pet-oriented parodies.

AN ANIMAL-RIGHTS ADVOCATE MIGHT ASK, IS IT FAIR TO IMBUE THE PIG WITH ALL THESE NEGATIVE QUALITIES? PIGS ARE ACTUALLY WONDERFUL CREATURES. Pigs are quite clean and smart, that's true. We exploited their symbolic

PLAYBOY—THE PARODY MAGAZINE
PARODY, 1984
ART DIRECTOR/DESIGNER: DAVID KAESTLE
PHOTOGRAPHER: JOHN DEREK
CLIENT: TAYLOR SCHAINE

image, you might say, for our purposes. Regardless, *Sty* was not a blockbuster, because the host publication didn't have enough readers to support a parody. If virtually every reader of *Spy* had bought *Sty*, it still would have failed. It was not cheap to produce.

YOU SAID THAT <u>STY</u> WORKED ON VARIOUS LEVELS. HOW DO YOU CONCEIVE AND THEN CARRY OUT YOUR GOAL OF MAKING A MULTI-LAYERED SATIRE? It's not principally a design problem; it's more an issue of editorial concept. There must be a very strong premise from which everything proceeds. Then the writers have to understand just how to create their subject matter with just the right sensibilities. Very, very few people are good at it, others are not. That's why most parodies don't work very well.

Let's jump to an example of genre parody. I designed a book called *The Pentagon Catalog* for Workman Publishers, at the height of the controversy about government overspending on faulty weapons systems and spare parts. It was a mock mail-order catalog, but not a parody of anything specific. We simply wanted to achieve a kind of low-budget mail-order sensibility, and we borrowed from all sorts of catalogs to do it. We knew that we could not photograph or afford the fabrication of props for this "expensive" stuff—most of the material was impossible to obtain anyway—so we had an artist draw it. The drawings were based on real sources. The products, price, and part and government ID numbers were all true, but the copy was a hoax. The point is that the book is only half a falsehood—that's why its so acerbic. Henry Beard, who, along with Chris Cerf, as the author, refers to the genre as investigative satire.

FOR PARODY OR SATIRE TO HAVE A STRONG IMPACT, IT HAS TO BE ROOTED IN THE TRUTH. If you stray too far from what seems to be believable, then the reader discards the entire thing as too far off the mark.

WHAT IS THE MOST SUCCESSFUL PARODY THAT YOU HAVE WORKED ON? *The National Lampoon High School Yearbook* parody, which sold in the millions.

COULD THAT KIND OF PARODY BE SUCCESSFUL TODAY? I don't think so. The yearbook came out before *Saturday Night Live* and before the stand-up comedy revolution. The humor landscape changes like everything else, maybe a little bit faster. In 1974, a lampoon of a 1964 yearbook was incredibly fresh and sassy. It was basically masterminded by P. J. O'Rourke and Doug Kenney. And Kenney, who was absolutely brilliant, never forgot anything that happened to him in high school.

WHY WAS THE YEARBOOK THEME CHOSEN? IS IT BECAUSE KENNEY HAD A HORRIFIC MEMORY OF HIS SCHOOL DAYS? It was a spin-off of a piece in the monthly [*National Lampoon*]

NATIONAL LAMPOON HIGH SCHOOL
YEARBOOK PARODY, 1974
ART DIRECTOR/DESIGNER:
DAVID KAESTLE
PHOTOGRAPHER: VINCE AIOSA
CLIENT: NATIONAL LAMPOON

STY MAGAZINE PARODY, 1989
ART DIRECTOR/DESIGNER:
DAVID KAESTLE
PHOTOGRAPHERS: DICK FRANK,
JOHN E. BARRETT
CLIENT: VINTAGE

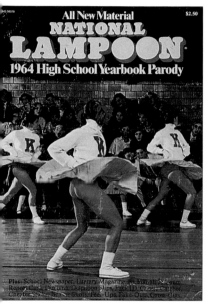

magazine, consisting of about eight pages of stuff. And we just felt it was a natural book idea. *Lampoon* readers, and editors, in fact, were young, and they had vivid memories of high school. It was an ordeal from their recent past.

The editors feared that it couldn't be sustained for 150 pages, so in fact the book is only about 90 pages of yearbook parody with the rest parodies of the school newspapers, literary magazines, and assorted other things. We cast kids from a New York private school to be the students in our "Central School" in Dacron, Ohio. We had to come up with sports and band uniforms and all the other requisite paraphernalia. then we shot photographs at least three days a week for nine weeks. Two stylists worked full-time dressing people and doing hair in vintage 1964 styles.

AS YOU WERE DOING THIS, DID YOU HAVE THE SENSE OF HOW FUNNY IT WAS GOING TO BE? Yes! We knew we had a winner from day one. We would bring the contact sheets back to the office, and people would just double up laughing.

ON WHAT DID YOU BASE THE DESIGN SCHEME? A composite of about 40 high school yearbooks from all over the country. It was quite easy, since they all looked alike. The design strategy from then on became a matter of how many rules could we break. One artist did all the graphics—those stupidly drawn headings, like *Faculty* and *Yearbook Staff*, etc.

DO YOU THINK IT STILL HOLDS UP AFTER SO MANY YEARS? I can still pick it up and laugh. It was so successful that *Lampoon* decided to make the movie *Animal House*. Essentially, the movie was the *High School Yearbook* parody off to college.

DESPITE SOME VERY SHARP HUMOR, THE LAMPOON AND ITS OFFSHOOTS WERE NOT MEAN-SPIRITED. BUT THERE SEEMS TO BE A TREND IN MEAN-SPIRITED HUMOR TODAY. DO YOU THINK IT'S SELF-DEFEATING? I don't quite know what you mean by self-defeating. If it's wildly successful, if people want it, then it's not self-defeating. But that doesn't make it funny. Andrew Dice Clay is mean-spirited, I'd say, and he's very successful, at least for now. But I don't think he's *funny*. *Outrageous*, yes, *bold*, yes; *funny*, rarely.

I like humor with an edge, with a point to make or an axe to grind. But that does not give license to be *only* pointed—being funny is always the prerequisite.

FORREST AND VALERIE RICHARDSON ARE PRINCIPALS OF RICHARDSON DESIGN IN PHOENIX

HOW IS HUMOR INCLUDED IN YOUR WORK? **VR:** It depends on the problem. Humor or wit can be part of the solution. But it is not the only way we try to solve problems . . . **FR:** But we do use humor more. And there are a couple of reasons for that. First, we're pretty fun people; we like humor . . . **VR:** Yet I don't think we're *funny* people. **FR:** You're right! But we enjoy having fun. We're outgoing, and we like to entertain. In fact, someone once said that a graphic designer is part entertainer. I agree. For example, when you go out to a restaurant, a menu should entertain to a certain degree . . . **VR:** But it could entertain and still *not* be funny.

YET THE IDEA OF ENTERTAINMENT SUGGESTS THAT YOU ARE, IF NOT OVERTLY HUMOROUS, NEVERTHELESS LIGHTHEARTED IN YOUR APPROACH. **FR:** Disneyland has influenced the way that I work. I was born in the year that it opened. And since I grew up in Southern California, I've been to Disneyland probably more than any other human being, so I know the park inside and out. And Valerie was exposed to similar environments in Coney Island. Another thing that had an influence on both of us is the fact that we both write. We've always believed that there's a distinct advantage to writing and designing from the same mind, because it affords you the opportunity to stop looking at copy as just a nice gray tone that happens to be included in a design. **VR:** We look at type as type, not as "copy."

OBVIOUSLY, THAT IMPLIES THAT YOU WANT FULL CONTROL OF YOUR DESIGN PROJECTS. AND HAVING CONTROL OF THE VERBAL LANGUAGE IS INDEED POWERFUL. BUT CAN SOMETHING BE DESIGNED SO THAT HUMOR IS INHERENT IN THE DESIGN ALONE? OR MUST YOU HAVE A MARRIAGE OF WORD AND IMAGE? **FR:** We designed a poster made up of the fingerprints of all sorts of people—from Helen Gurly Brown to Saul Bass—for a printer called Heritage Graphics. The tagline is actually a rather serious comment: "If the greatest gift of all is life, then the second must be that no two are alike." Yet despite its serious intent, I consider solutions like that to be witty because they are a surprise, and what's put on the page is not easily understood with a brief passing. In the thumbprint poster, there are elements that require more contemplation than overtly illustrative posters to get the full impact of the idea. Some people might not take the time to get it. But for those who do, it's vexing to raise questions like, "Why would someone do this?" After all, it's just a printing promotion.

BUT IT <u>IS</u> EYE- AND PERHAPS MIND-CATCHING. AND ISN'T THAT WHAT GOOD ADVERTISING, NO LESS GOOD GRAPHIC DESIGN, IS ALL ABOUT? **FR:** Yes. And we did something equally bizarre as a New Year's promotion for a photographer. It was a bunch of perforated squares on a huge poster that otherwise looked rather elegant. It was printed in solid red on both sides with three

LOWERCASE NUMERALS CHART, 1989
ART DIRECTORS/DESIGNERS:
FORREST AND VALERIE RICHARDSON
COPYWRITER: FORREST RICHARDSON
CLIENT: KANSAS CITY ART
DIRECTORS CLUB

THUMBPRINT POSTER, 1988
ART DIRECTORS: FORREST AND
VALERIE RICHARDSON
COPYWRITER: FORREST RICHARDSON
CLIENT: HERITAGE GRAPHICS

hundred feet of perforated rules—one entire football field of rules—cutting the piece into a grid. The idea was, you rip this up, and when you were done, there were 1,990 individual little squares of confetti to toss on New Year's Eve.

THOUGH YOU'RE DESCRIBING IT IN PRINTING TERMS, THIS IS NOT REALLY A DESIGN JOKE. I SUGGEST THIS BECAUSE THERE ARE MANY FORMS OF VISUAL HUMOR THAT ARE JUST TOO ARCANE FOR THE PUBLIC BECAUSE THEY ARE IN-JOKES, MEANT EXCLUSIVELY FOR DESIGNERS. DO YOU TRY TO BE MORE GENERAL AS A RULE? FR: I like fooling people. Sometimes my humor is for everyone, other times not. For one project, we created a mythical company—which *is* a design joke—called the Az You Like It Type Foundry. It began as an announcement for ourselves when we speak at art directors' clubs and conferences. On occasion, we are asked to create a poster. So rather than one that says, "Des Moines Is Great and So Are We," our poster is about a mythical business that caters to the love of kitsch in us all.

WHY IS THE NAIVE CONSIDERED SO FUNNY? AS PROFESSIONAL DESIGNERS, WE TEND TO LOOK AT THAT OLD-FASHIONED "COMMERCIAL ART" WITH A CERTAIN AMOUNT OF DERISION—IS THAT WHY IT IS FUNNY? FR: Velvet paintings are the same way . . . **VR:** It's not derision—you could really use some of these things as part of a well-designed idea, and have some fun at the same time. **FR:** And it would be cost-efficient.

You pay the guy a hundred dollars, he'd work all day . . .

BUT WHY IS THAT FUNNY? FR: The reason it's funny to designers—and maybe to no one else—is that it goes contrary to the norm. And that in itself is more exciting than going to a reference book and hiring a professional illustrator or typographer. But it's funny to *everyone* only if it's used the right way.

ONE OF THE POSTERS FOR YOUR MYTHICAL TYPE FOUNDRY IS BASED ON "LOWERCASE" NUMERALS. WHAT A SUBTLE BIT OF SATIRE. HOW DID THAT COME ABOUT? FR: Well, it's actually not too far-fetched and could be very useful. **VR:** Come on, Forrest, how could it be useful? **FR:** Actually, the more I thought about it over the last several years, the more I realized it *is* pretty stupid. But many people didn't realize it was a joke and have asked me where to get them.

BY VIRTUE OF THE ELEGANT TYPOGRAPHY AND FINE PRINTING, THE POSTER WAS "STRAIGHT-FACED." THAT WOULD INDUCE PEOPLE—LIKE ME—TO THINK IT WAS FOR REAL. HOW DO YOU RECONCILE THE SOPHISTICATED GRAPHIC APPROACH WITH A HUMOROUS IDEA? FR: It comes down to appropriateness. **VR:** We try to design an image that will intrigue the viewers and, as Forrest said earlier, occasionally fool them. A well-crafted piece will get and hold attention. But most important, and perhaps it's true with all our work, we don't want them to get the joke right away. Let it sneak up on them and they'll appreciate it more.

RICK VALICENTI IS THE PRINCIPAL OF THIRST IN CHICAGO

HOW IS HUMOR REPRESENTED IN YOUR WORK? I don't usually set out to do something funny, just as I don't intentionally do something ugly, but sometimes it turns out that way. No matter what it is, my intention is to do something as pretty as possible. Yet it never looks like everybody else's concept of pretty. I also try to do it straight, but it always comes out bent.

WHAT DO YOU MEAN BY BENT? A little twisted. The more I design, the more I discover that so much of it is truly an extension of my personality. So I'm learning a lot about myself as I work.

LET'S TALK MORE ABOUT THAT PART OF YOUR PERSONALITY THAT'S TWISTED. HOW DOES THIS "DEFECT" ENTER INTO YOUR WORK? On the surface, most people would say that I'm a pretty normal guy. I have two kids and live in the Chicago suburbs. I'm not a fashion plate. But I would characterize myself as a 39-year-old who still thinks he's 14. During client meetings, I act like an adult. But my work during the design process seems to be more childlike. More curious. More excitable. Visually very happy!

I UNDERSTAND THAT YOU ENTERED DESIGN THROUGH THE BACK DOOR. I'm not a trained designer. I got into this profession by doing keylines at a recruitment ad agency. After doing graduate work in photography—I have two graduate degrees—I came to Chicago. Not wanting to shoot hot dogs for a living, I entered the design business doing ad borders and was taught how to use a ruling pen. So today I'm fascinated with ornamentation of all kinds.

GIVEN THIS RATHER TECHNICAL BEGINNING, YOUR WORK, THOUGH VISUALLY COMPLEX, DOES NOT SEEM LABORED. Most things are very spontaneous. I always say "I can do that," regardless of how busy I am. Hence, we're always overbooked. There is never any time for total design resolution, so the lack of time has sort of become a "look."

Let me give you an example. I did a poster for a benefit called "The Joker Is Wild," a little bash promoting a deck of designer playing cards produced by the American Center for Design. I could have run everybody's card on the poster, but that was too easy. I'm not certain why I had a vision of Joel Grey in *Cabaret,* but it became an overriding fixation for me, and so I wanted to make the poster have a simi-

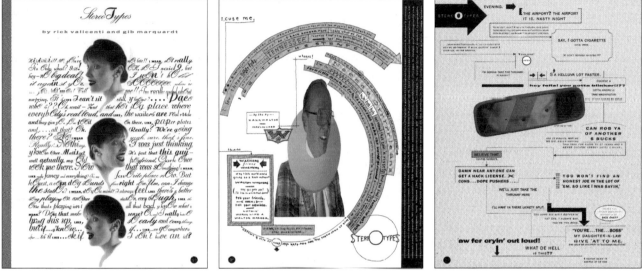

lar aesthetic as that of Grey in that Berlin cabaret. I had also just seen a preview for the film *The Last Emperor,* which had a quick cut of a woman's face painted white with a red dot over her lips—very striking. So I went home and drew a woman standing in what was akin to a Steve Martin white suit, without a shirt, holding a microphone, wearing a fake bow tie and little top hat—like Grey—with an arrow through her head. To me, this was a wild joker stuck in some time warp. When it came out, people thought it was far afield. But I thought it was a pretty good interpretation of the title, "The Joker Is Wild."

HAVE YOU HAD PROBLEMS GETTING YOUR OFF-THE-WALL NOTIONS ACCEPTED BY CLIENTS? I've been fortunate that our clients are very supportive.

ONE OF THE WEIRDER PIECES YOU'VE DONE IS SOMETHING CALLED "STEREOTYPES." CAN YOU DESCRIBE THE GENESIS OF THIS? I was invited by *Step-By-Step Graphics* magazine to show some of my work in a special issue devoted to typography. Rather than show yet another portfolio, I suggested that they run something original, done for the magazine. And so "Stereotypes" was born.

I focused in on auditory typography, exploring whether or not different typefaces embodied different personalities. Or could different types have specific sounds—like that of a young woman or a gruff old guy. We know what Cooper Black looks like, but what does it really *sound* like? What does Univers 47 sound like? What does the person look like who made the sound of Univers 47?

The editor of *Step-By-Step* had invited me to preview my work at the 1989 Graphix convention in New York City. I decided to do a multimedia presentation based on the notion of taking four characters who had a certain forceful presence and letting them speak through type. They were what I call stereotypical characters: a

"IND'FENCE" (FRONT AND BACK)
PROGRAM-ANNOUNCEMENT POSTER, 1990
DESIGNER/COPYWRITER: RICK VALICENTI/THIRST
CLIENT: AIGA/SAN FRANCISCO

manicurist, taxi driver, blind date, and sales-man—you know, the kind who sits next to you on an airplane and won't shut up. For the first, I had a paragraph of text generated by a writer, spoken by a friend in the back of a taxi, while I videotaped a real cab driver making hand ges-tures, as if he were speaking. Then I created 10 "type draw-ings," concrete in composition, auditory in emphasis and pac-ing. At my Graphix preview, I showed the videotape of the cab-bie along with slides of the type. **YOU MEAN LIKE SUBTITLES, EXCEPT IN THIS CASE YOU USED WORDS MADE OF EXPRES-SIVE TYPE?** It was more like the old "follow the bouncing ball." When it was over, Paula Scher commented, somewhat critically, that it was "just Dada." Other than the fact that the drawings had a typographic texture, they

had nothing to do with Dada—they were much too controlled, Her comment, however, made me want to try a more random process and let that dictate the final look of the printed piece. The randomness made it more compelling. **SOME FUNNY IDEAS ARE BEST UNPREMEDITAT-ED; OTHERS ARE FINE-TUNED FOR MAXIMUM EFFECT. HOW DID THE PRINTED VERSION OF "STEREOTYPES" ULTIMATELY COME INTO BEING?** It was rather free-form. For the first one, the blind date lady, we photographed a model and I colorized her hair electronically. I drew boxes indicating where the typesetter should set

type, selecting ten script faces in his library that I wanted him to use. However, I wanted every *o* to be set in the same font. I wanted the word *like,* which came up often, to be set the same size and in a contrasting font throughout. But I told the typesetter to make all the other decisions himself; he could decide whether a face should change according to syl-lable or more randomly. He could change a font or the point size, wherever he wanted, as long as it filled the box. I didn't want to know why he made the decision, but I did say that if he wanted to come up with an overriding scheme, he could—I would print whatever came from the experiment without any "design edit." But, you know, it's not easy for a typesetter to func-tion without specifications. So the pain was fun to watch.

Some people think I spec-ced the type, because some of the relationships between letterforms are very beautiful, but on the whole it's kind of ugly. The typesetter took what are stereotypically perceived as beautiful—feminine faces—and then, by jamming them together, gave them a new personality and voice. Like any voice, it has highs and lows, squeals and rants, and quiet moments too. But the result was really ugly by my standards. **BUT APPROPRIATELY UGLY, PERHAPS?** Many things are contradictory. Fire can be good and bad. So can water and air. Form can be simulta-neously beautiful and ugly. The taxi piece in this series was in that mold. I cut up a book of German Berthold type and made a very quick collage. In fact, many of the printed rules were actually the cut edges of the paper that emerged when I xeroxed the collage. I sent all this gobbledy-gook to the typesetter along with the manuscript. I told him that I wanted it to look this way but that *he* would have to figure out how the words should break in order to make sense. He did it quite well.

The *National Enquirer* piece was also a spontaneous collage of headlines and body copy from a real *Enquirer*. Again, I sent the paste-up to the typesetter with the manuscript and told him to make it look like the sketch with the color break just as it was. I also wanted him to give me as much of the bad type character as possible—

President Dwight D. Eisenhower celebrated his 66th birthday with a cake that made it into the newspapers.

PRESIDENT EISENHOWER'S

which he was unable to do on his system, since his kerning patterns are just too strict and his fonts are too beautiful to really make them look that ugly. Nevertheless, the parody of Berthold type in the form of the *National Enquirer* amuses me.

WHAT WAS THE STORY BEHIND THE HEADLINES OF THE ENQUIRER PIECE? We decided to take the most extreme version of Madge, the manicurist, and have her speak through the most popular force in contemporary English language. Hence, her voice was interpreted to be like headlines in the *National Enquirer*.

For the last one, the peanut salesman, I decided I would use one of my first unrevised sketches. Actually, I wanted the typesetter to set the type as it appeared on the finish. But he said it would take six hours to set, because each character would have to be set separately on the arc. So it occurred to me that I could just use my sketch as the finish, which would give the idea more backbone.

WHAT DO YOU FIND FUNNY ABOUT YOUR WORK? Maybe what is funny, or shall we say a little twisted, are the juxtapositions. The "Kitty Cage" poster, which I did as an announcement for a talk I gave in San Francisco, is an example of something I thought was hysterical. Because when the poster says "In Defense," this lady is in "the fence." It's based on Chicagoese, or Brooklynese, "da fence."

THERE IS SOMETHING NONSENSICAL ABOUT THIS IMAGE. IS THAT ITS ONLY REASON FOR BEING? It's just the kind of word- and image-play I love to do. I found the cage in the back of a friend's van. I discovered a doodle in the food section of the *Chicago Tribune* on Dwight Eisenhower's birthday. I started to think about these two seemingly unrelated minor discoveries and focused on their common properties. Simultaneity is my style. When I realized the relationship between side A ["in d'fense"] and side B ["on d'fense"], I flipped. How could I resist? It's like being a kid in a candy store, I guess.

STEVEN GUARNACCIA IS AN ILLUSTRATOR/DESIGNER BASED IN NEW YORK

WHAT MAKES YOUR WORK HUMOROUS? The way it's drawn has something to do with it. I try to make a piece look like the idea just occurred to me and in just that moment was committed to paper.

IS THE HUMOROUS LINE SOMETHING YOU STUDIED OR DID IT NATURALLY EVOLVE? I never considered myself a very good draftsman. So, in a way, it was an out for me. I worked to develop it, but I didn't purposefully switch from a more rendered approach to a lighter, wittier line.

WHAT IS IT ABOUT YOUR WORK THAT MAKES IT INHERENTLY FUNNY? When I began as an illustrator, what was funny about my line was its tenuousness—in the manner of R. O. Blechman's nervous line. That kind of shakiness is one of the qualities that I've gotten away from over the years, simply by switching tools—from rapidographs to fountain pens and even markers in some cases. Today, the basis of my humorous line is just the opposite, because, rather than tenuous, it's fluid and quick. Whatever the approach, it's necessary that the result look handmade. The line must have a distinct personality.

SO THE WEIGHT OF HUMOR DOES NOT REST ON THE LINE ALONE? No. Odd or unexpected juxtapositions have always interested me. And one of the techniques I've used over the years is a scale shift—making large things incredibly small and small things grotesquely large.

IS HUMOR INHERENT IN ANY LARGE/SMALL RELATIONSHIP? Of course, there are enlargements that become too grotesque and diminutions that become too cute. It's up to the judgment of the individual artist.

AT WHAT POINT DOES AN IDEA THAT SEEMS GENUINELY FUNNY IN YOUR MIND BECOME TOO GROTESQUE OR CUTE ON PAPER? In the early days, I rarely imagined things the way I would draw them. I didn't have a mastery of the craft, and when I would think of an idea, that idea had an existence apart from my drawing of it. I realized that when they would misfire, they weren't really *my* ideas—I didn't really own them technically or stylistically. Now I only think of ideas that I can successfully draw in my style. The times I misfire are either because every now and then I think of an idea that I really shouldn't be doing, or because it's a joke only I appreciate.

DO YOU MEAN AN IN-JOKE? A joke between myself and me. Like when certain things strike me as funny but the person next to me doesn't get it. As an example, I do a monthly "featurette" for *Metropolitan Home* that I write and illustrate. It's not my usual responsive mode, where I read an article and react, which is like playing off a straight man.

THAT'S AN INTERESTING DESCRIPTION. IS THAT HOW YOU FEEL WHEN YOU ARE ILLUSTRAT-

FACING PAGE: <u>PEARL'S PROGRESS</u>
BOOK JACKET, 1989
ART DIRECTOR: CAROL CARSON
ILLUSTRATOR: STEVEN GUARNACCIA
CLIENT: ALFRED A. KNOPF

HOME TRUTHS SERIES, 1989–1991
ART DIRECTOR: DON MORRIS
ILLUSTRATOR: STEVEN GUARNACCIA
CLIENT: <u>METROPOLITAN HOME</u>

"MEAT DISTRICT" MOVING
ANNOUNCEMENT, 1988
ILLUSTRATOR:
STEVEN GUARNACCIA
CLIENT: SELF

ING—LIKE A COMEDIAN RESPONDING TO A STRAIGHT MAN, OR WOMAN? Some of the hardest work I have ever done was as the regular illustrator for Russell Baker's column in the *New York Times Magazine*. Here the roles were reversed. He was the funny man and I had a hard time being funnier than he was. The straight man analogy is apt, and I relished the opportunity of working against the dry articles in the financial section of the *New York Times*, because against those I could be the class clown.

THE <u>METROPOLITAN HOME</u> PIECES ARE ALL PUNS. IN FACT, YOU USE MANY VISUAL AND VERBAL PUNS IN YOUR WORK. RATHER THAN ASKING THE OBVIOUS, TELL ME ABOUT SOME OF THE MOST UNSUCCESSFUL PUNS. I know there's nothing worse than a painful pun. One of those was under the heading "Shaker Table," which showed two huge salt shakers propping up a pane of glass. I think I'll probably redraw this one and make it a situational gag—that might make it funnier. I guess the reason it worked so poorly is that any joke needs to engage the reader on other levels than just the wordplay. I did

another called "Armoir," showing a closet of arms. It didn't work because there was no reverberation. There's no reason for anyone to stay with the idea. By comparison, I did one called "Infantile," which was quite successful. It's a picture of the corner of a child's room; you see just the leg of a crib, next to a little ball lying on the floor, and there are alternating tiles of little baby faces and letters of the alphabet. It's a checkerboard floor, and all the colors are soft pastels. This one works on a lot of different levels: The word *infantile* actually means what this picture is about. If you break it down into component parts, *infant* and *tile* each have resonance.

HOW DO YOU EXPECT YOUR AUDIENCE TO REACT TO THIS PIECE? I want the viewer's participation. I want them to put in the same effort as I did in coming up with the idea.

IT DOESN'T SEEM LIKE MUCH TO ASK. IS ALL YOUR WORK HUMOR-BASED? Ten years ago I would have said no. That was a time when I was trying to be a lot of different illustrators in one. I was testing my ability, for instance, to be an op-ed–style conceptual illustrator. I had this humorous edge, but I was taking the work and myself too seriously. Today, I think I've abandoned the need to be taken so seriously, because I feel like humor is so important in life that all I have to do is be is funny to justify my existence as an artist.

-HOUSEDRESS-

APRIL GARSTEN AND ZOE BROTMAN ARE PARTNERS IN ICON DESIGN, NEW YORK CITY

WHAT CHEMISTRY BROUGHT YOU TOGETHER AS PARTNERS? AG: Caffeine. We had very strong tea one night and talked about starting a studio.

WHY IS HUMOR INTEGRAL TO YOUR WORK? AG: We don't like design that takes itself too seriously. Our ideas come from brainstorming. And brainstorming is when we loosen up and goof around. At some point, we start getting serious about the subject at hand, but we're already in a good mood. Of course, it also helps to have small clients that give us latitude. **ZB:** With our line of T-shirts, we didn't have to answer to a real client, so we could be as far-out as we wanted.

WERE THE T-SHIRTS ORIGINALLY A COMMERCIAL PROJECT? ZB: We did four styles of T-shirts for Earth Day 1990 and sold eight hundred in one day alone. We were astonished and so inspired to try our hands at a new medium. We had talked about doing products for a while—like so many designers do—because we wanted to explore directions other than two-dimensional design. It's rewarding to do a product, because you just invent the wheel once and then, if it's good, it sells continuously.

WHERE DID THE IDEA FOR THESE T-SHIRTS COME FROM? ZB: We had a collection of eclectic imagery that inspired us. **AG:** Ideas just materialized. For one of the shirts, Zoe put down two strange images and I said, "That

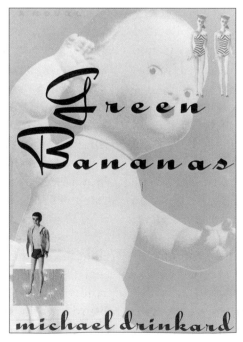

should say something like, '"Brocoli," he thought to himself.' Now let's think of a real line," and Zoe said, "That *was* the real line."

ZB: We didn't really have a theme. It was simply what we liked and thought might be marketable. We felt free to take chances with whatever came to mind, and didn't underestimate our audience.

HUMOR IS A PROBLEM FOR MANY CLIENTS. BUT YOU HAVE CLIENTS WHO APPARENTLY CALL ON YOU ESPECIALLY FOR YOUR WHIMSY. WHY DO YOU SUPPOSE THAT'S THE CASE? ZB: Probably because many of our clients are in the entertainment field, and entertainment is about fun. **AG:** Generally, they believe that the humorous approach will attract the right audience.

SPEAKING OF HOOKING AN AUDIENCE WITH WIT AS BAIT, YOU DID THE BOOK JACKET FOR GREEN BANANAS IN WHICH YOU JUXTAPOSED QUITE A FEW ODDBALL ELEMENTS. AG: It was a satiric first novel. We wanted to express something about the subject and tone of the book, and developed a collage of found and original images that related in a very strange way. It was a story about a lesbian couple. One of them wanted a baby and had her sights on a young college student working in a day-care center. So we used a "Ken" doll sitting in a little sea of sperm. Over his head was the head of a big baby doll. And then next to that were two les-

FACING PAGE: GREEN BANANAS BOOK
JACKET, 1989
ART DIRECTOR: CAROL CARSON
DESIGNERS: APRIL GARSTEN,
ZOE BROTMAN, ICON DESIGN
CLIENT: ALFRED A. KNOPF

T-SHIRTS, 1990
ART DIRECTORS/DESIGNERS:
APRIL GARSTEN, ZOE BROTMAN
CLIENT: ICON DESIGN

bian "Barbies." **ZB:** This was a case where our brand of visual humor was well-matched to the author's sensibility. You can judge this book by its cover.

HOW DID YOU WORK ON THIS TOGETHER? AG: We talked about what the ideas might be. In this case, we both had different inspirations. Then we broke off in our directions, going back and forth from time to time. We are ultimately inspired by each other.

DO YOU END UP WITH ONE PIECE PHYSICALLY MADE BY BOTH OF YOU? AG: There is no rule.

DO YOU USE FOUND OBJECTS A LOT? AG: By default, yes. We have a number of clients who don't have a budget for commissioning illustrations or photography. So naturally, we try to find free art that might already be in the studio. It's another way of loosening up our work.

YOUR STUDIO IS KIND OF LIKE A JUNK SHOP. ZB: I wouldn't say that. But we do have a lot of things we call "tricks." In fact, that's the title on one of our flat files that includes textures and images from old magazines, and strange type specimens—lots of different things that we just throw into it, like cooking a stew. It's a good way to start a project, especially if you don't have a clear-cut idea. We like to surround ourselves with lots of inspirations, whether we use them or not.

DO YOU DISTINGUISH BETWEEN PLAY AND HUMOR? AG: If I had to distinguish, I would say that humor is like being told a joke; play is like being tickled. **ZB:** At the end of our design process, we always ask ourselves whether the piece has the twist it needs. There is always one last element that will send it over the edge and make it transcend the ordinary.

CAN YOU GIVE AN EXAMPLE OF WHERE YOUR WIT CAME THROUGH EVEN THOUGH THE ASSIGNMENT WAS NOT NECESSARILY HUMOROUS? AG: We did a cover for a book about Andy Warhol. There was nothing inherently funny about the subject, but we did some subtle manipulations that tickled our fancy. We angled things, chose an offbeat color combination, and blew up Warhol's head so close you could see his pores. **ZB:** That in itself was amusing and playful.

YOU TOOK AN ICON AND PLAYED AROUND WITH IT. ZB: But even if it was a book about an unknown, I still think it would have the same visual wit. Of course, having it be Warhol helps.

CAN YOU DEFINE A PERSONAL STYLE? AG: I want to bring something new to each piece I design. That is why I like to work in a variety of styles. Each project may have a different look, but I always want it to have energy. **ZB:** I like taking an element from left field and making it seem like it always belonged there. My favorite projects are of the type where I can join the absurd and the sublime. I guess I would also say we're both a little twisted, but very nice girls.

ELWOOD H. SMITH IS AN ILLUSTRATOR
BASED IN RHINEBECK, NEW YORK.

IN ONE OF YOUR PROMOTIONAL ADVERTISE- MENTS YOU ASK THE QUESTION, "DOES BEING FUNNY PAY?" WELL, DOES IT? Yup.

WOULD YOU LIKE TO EXPAND ON THAT? When I was a little kid, I found that doing drawings was the way I could get through life. I was shy. I didn't do much of anything well. But I liked the comics and discovered I could draw in a similar fashion. I had whimsy in my work. And so, it became my way of being accepted by the other kids. Eventually, it made me feel more confident.

CAN YOU EXPLAIN WHAT THE WORD <u>WHIMSY</u> MEANS TO YOU? It simply means seeing the lighter side of things. My humor has never been dark. I've never been a practical joker, and I don't care for slapstick or laughs at the expense of others.

YOUR HUMOR IS KINDER AND GENTLER. Yes. And though I hate to refer to it this way, whimsy is more intellectual and less physical.

I GUESS FRIENDLY IS THE KEY. BUT WHY IS THE CONVENTION OF EXAGGERATING BELLIES, NOSES, FEET, HANDS, OR ANY OTHER AP- PENDAGE SO FUNNY? I can't tell you. But I do know that people do look like the characters I draw. I actually exaggerate only a little. Caricaturists, on the other hand, do it best and more profoundly. When you see a great carica- ture of Richard Nixon by David Levine, with those sharp, pointy teeth and five-o'clock shad- ow, it looks more like him than any photograph. My work is not as direct. The police could not use my drawings to find a fugitive, but neverthe- less my characters look like how I feel certain people *should* look. By the way, I am very near- sighted—the kind where if I take off my glasses, everything a foot away becomes a blur, but if I get within six inches of your face, you become so magnified I can see pores and hairs on the end of your nose. Well, that's exactly what my charac- ters look like. Many have little "pickers" stick- ing out all over them. It's just the way I see things.

YOU MEAN TO TELL ME THAT YOUR CHARAC- TERS ARE COMPOSITES OF THE WAY YOU SEE WITHOUT YOUR GLASSES? Not entirely. There's a certain amount of imagination in there too. But

SELF-PROMOTIONAL PAGES,
1989–1990
DESIGNER/ILLUSTRATOR:
ELWOOD H. SMITH
CLIENT: SELF

most important, cartoonists simply like to exaggerate things—stretching and pulling things into odd shapes. I don't know why that makes characters funny or lovable—it's just the way it is. People love babies, human and animal, and they have exaggerated features.

WHEN YOU ARE GIVEN AN ASSIGNMENT, THE ASSUMPTION IS THAT YOU ARE GOING TO RESPOND WITH WIT. IT'S NOT THAT I DON'T THINK WIT CANNOT BE USED TO COMMUNICATE SIGNIFICANT SOCIAL ISSUES, BUT GIVEN YOUR WHIMSICAL STYLE, I HOPE THAT AN ART DIRECTOR HAS NEVER ASKED YOU TO TACKLE HOMELESSNESS OR AIDS. WHAT ARE SOME OF THE BEST- AND WORST-CASE SCENARIOS IN YOUR CLIENT/ARTIST RELATIONS? Art directors often say to me, "We have a job that is perfectly *you*," or, "I've been a fan of your work for years and I've been waiting to work with you and have finally found a job you are going to love." Sometimes, when the job arrives, it's not so *me* after all.

WHAT DOES THAT MEAN? In advertising, the first warning sign is that the job is indicated or roughed out in someone else's style, and has already been sold to the client. From the outset, it is the art director's *interpretation* of what I do. And one key phrase that come's with this kind of assignment is, "have fun." Those two little words have little meaning anymore, although the occasional advertising art director allows me creative latitude.

WHAT RESULTS FROM TOTAL FREEDOM? Lots of things. Like the self-promotional ad I

did, called "Kartoon Korse: How to Draw Just Like E. H. Smith." I decided that I wanted to do something just to have fun, and thought that I was already well-known enough to take a risk in American Showcase. If my little indulgence didn't work—if I didn't generate any work from the ad—I'd be out $3,000. But I did get work from it. In fact, several of the assignments gave me the chance to use the same off-the-wall approach I used in my self-promotional piece.

WHEN YOU SPEAK OF OFF-THE-WALL HUMOR, I ASSUME YOU MEAN UNINHIBITED HUMOR. IF SO, HOW DOES THIS HAPPEN? WHERE DO THE IDEAS FOR CHARACTERS AND SITUATIONS COME FROM? I always doodle when I'm on the phone, and I paste the best of them in a sketchbook. These stream-of-consciousness drawings spark up my commercial work. I equate my process with being a jazz, as opposed to a classical, musician. With the latter, everything is perfectly buttoned down, and then he

might creatively interpret a particular piece. The jazz player comes to a piece with great skill, but the music unfolds at the very moment it's happening.

AS A CARTOONIST, YOU USE CERTAIN STEREO-TYPES. HOW DO YOU AVOID PERPETUATING INSENSITIVE CLICHÉS? By being sensitive to them. For instance, I hardly ever choose to put women in my drawings, not because I am anti-women—I'm definitely not—but because I like

drawing little round fat people with bald heads covered with little pickers sticking out. These could be women, but in advertising and women's magazines, the demand is for "unoffensive" or "attractive" females. So I comply. I repeat, my humor is not mean-spirited, I do not intentionally use stereotypes to hurt anyone.

DOES YOUR HUMOR REQUIRE A MARRIAGE OF WORD AND PICTURE, OR CAN YOU SUCCEED WITH PICTURES ALONE? I used to use pure images to illustrate a manuscript. Then, slowly, I began to allow words to creep into my drawings to augment or clarify the idea I was trying to convey. I thought, if my favorite cartoonists use "talk balloons," why shouldn't I?.

IS FREEDOM THE KEY TO MAKING GOOD HUMOR? If I don't free myself, or I'm not allowed to be free in the sense of having a fresh interpretation of my characters, the client ends up with a worse job than if I could improvise. I cannot understand why some clients do not let me have that leeway. I'm sure I do my best work that way. And the closer they let me come to my personal work, the more they get for their money.

My latest promotional ad even says something to that effect. It's a list of rules to follow: "Make sure I'm right for the assignment. Give me lots of creative freedom, and you'll get your money's worth—guaranteed." And that's no joke!

WE SPOKE ABOUT WORDS AND PICTURES. LET'S JUST FOCUS ON THE FORM THAT YOUR WORDS TAKE. INDEED, WHAT MAKES YOUR LETTERING SO FUNNY? I guess part of what makes my lettering funny is the fact that it has the same energy as my line. Still, I can't tell you why my line is funny, and maybe I shouldn't even try.